ROYAL
FAMILY ALBUM

Produced by

TED SMART & DAVID GIBBON

Text by

DON COOLICAN

MAYFLOWER BOOKS, INC.,
NEW YORK 10022.

Pietro Annigoni's famous portrait of the
Queen was commissioned by the Worshipful
Company of Fishmongers. It now hangs in
the Fishmonger Hall in the City of London.

The Line of Descent of Queen Elizabeth II

CERDIC, first king of the West Saxons (d.534)
|
Crioda
|
CYNRIC (534–560)
|
CEAWLIN (560–591)
|
Cuthwine (d. 584)
|
Cuthwulf
|
Ceolwald
|
Cenred, under-king of Sussex (692)
|
Ingild (d. 718), brother of King Ine
|
Eoppa
|
Eaba
|
Ealhmund, under-king of Kent (786)

EGBERT = Redburh
|
ETHELWULF = Osburh (1st wife)
|
ALFRED THE GREAT = Ealhswith
|
EDWARD = Edgiva (3rd wife)
|
EDMUND I = Elgiva (1st wife)
|
EDGAR = Elfrida (2nd wife)
|
ETHELRED II THE UNREADY = Elfleda (1st wife)
|
EDMUND II IRONSIDE = Ealdgyth
|
Edward Atheling the Exile = Agatha
|
St. Margaret = Malcolm III of Scotland

WILLIAM I (the Conqueror) = Matilda of Flanders
|
HENRY I = Matilda (1st wife)
|
Geoffrey, Count of Anjou = Matilda
|
HENRY II = Eleanor of Aquitaine
|
JOHN = Isabella of Angoulême (2nd wife)
|
HENRY III = Eleanor of Provence
|
EDWARD I = Eleanor of Castile (1st wife)
|
EDWARD II = Isabella of France
|
EDWARD III = Philippa of Hainault

John of Gaunt, Duke of Lancaster = Katharine Swynford (3rd wife)
Edmund, Duke of York = Isabel of Castile (1st wife)

John, Marquess of Dorset = Margaret Holland
Richard, Earl of Cambridge = Anne Mortimer

John Beaufort, Duke of Somerset = Margaret Beauchamp
Richard, Duke of York = Cecily Neville

Edmund Tudor, Earl of Richmond = Margaret Beaufort
EDWARD IV = Elizabeth Woodville

HENRY VII = Elizabeth of York

James IV of Scotland = Margaret Tudor
HENRY VIII = Anne Boleyn (2nd wife)

James V of Scotland = Mary of Lorraine
ELIZABETH I

Mary, Queen of Scots = Henry Stuart, Lord Darnley (2nd husband)
|
JAMES I = Anne of Denmark
|
Frederick, King of Bohemia = Elizabeth Stuart
|
Ernest Augustus, Elector of Hanover = Sophia
|
GEORGE I = Sophia Dorothea of Celle
|
GEORGE II = Caroline of Brandenburg-Anspach
|
Frederick Lewis, Prince of Wales = Augusta of Saxe-Gotha
|
GEORGE III = Charlotte of Mecklenburg-Strelitz
|
Edward, Duke of Kent = Victoria of Saxe-Coburg-Saalfeld
|
VICTORIA = Albert of Saxe-Coburg and Gotha (Prince Consort)
|
EDWARD VII = Alexandra of Denmark
|
GEORGE V = Mary of Teck
|
GEORGE VI = The Lady Elizabeth Bowes-Lyon
|
QUEEN ELIZABETH II = The Prince Philip, Duke of Edinburgh

Charles, Prince of Wales   The Princess Anne   The Prince Andrew   The Prince Edward

Britain's Sovereigns

William I	1066–1087
William II	1087–1100
Henry I	1100–1135
Stephen	1135–1154
Henry II	1154–1189
Richard I	1189–1199
John	1199–1216
Henry III	1216–1272
Edward I	1272–1307
Edward II	1307–1327
Edward III	1327–1377
Richard II	1377–1399
Henry IV	1399–1413
Henry V	1413–1422
Henry VI	1422–1461
Edward IV	1461–1483
Edward V	1483
Richard III	1483–1485
Henry VII	1485–1509
Henry VIII	1509–1547
Edward VI	1547–1553
Jane Grey	1553
Mary I	1553–1558
Elizabeth I	1558–1603
James I	1603–1625
Charles I	1625–1649
Commonwealth Declared 1649	
Oliver Cromwell Lord Protector	1653–1658
Richard Cromwell Lord Protector	1658–1659
Charles II	1649–1685
James II	1685–1689
William III and Mary II	1689–1702 / 1689–1694
Anne	1702–1714
George I	1714–1727
George II	1727–1760
George III	1760–1820
George IV	1820–1830
William IV	1830–1837
Victoria	1837–1901
Edward VII	1901–1910
George V	1910–1936
Edward VIII	1936
George VI	1936–1952
Elizabeth II	Succeeded 1952

The Royal Line of Succession

1 H.R.H. The Prince of Wales (Heir Apparent)
2 H.R.H. The Prince Andrew
3 H.R.H. The Prince Edward
4 H.R.H. The Princess Anne
5 Master Peter Phillips
6 H.R.H. The Princess Margaret, Countess of Snowdon
7 Viscount Linley
8 Lady Sarah Armstrong-Jones
9 H.R.H. The Duke of Gloucester
10 The Earl of Ulster
11 H.R.H. The Duke of Kent
12 The Earl of St. Andrews
13 Lord Nicholas Windsor
14 Lady Helen Windsor
15 H.R.H. Prince Michael of Kent
16 H.R.H. Princess Alexandra, the Hon. Mrs Angus Ogilvy
17 Mr James Ogilvy
18 Miss Marina Ogilvy
19 The Earl of Harewood
20 Viscount Lascelles

CONTENTS

Left. The Royal Family – HM the Queen,
Prince Philip, Prince Charles, Princess Anne,
Prince Andrew and Prince Edward.
(Desmond Groves)

Introduction

by Don Coolican

It was King George VI who said: "We're not a family, we're a firm". Yet a long-serving member of the Royal Household once told me: "I never feel as if I'm working at Buckingham Palace – it's like being part of a very busy family".

Is Queen Elizabeth II merely the managing director of a company called "Royal Family Ltd" promoting Britain and the monarchy? Or is she the head of a group of kinsfolk, leading lives cut off from the rest of us, but who occasionally pop out of their palaces to wave to the masses?

To many people the royals seem to be slightly plastic figures from the world of glossy magazines, television newsreels and gossip columns: apparently protected from the problems of living we lesser mortals face: superstars who exist only in a world of pomp and privilege.

The aura which is with them at all times tends to cut them off from most men and women. They either hold, or will inherit, great titles, there is little uncertainty in their lives, and the problems of paying the monthly bills never bother them.

Yet with our tendency to hedge them in behind gold-painted gates, we can overlook that the House of Windsor is above all a family: wives, husbands, sons, daughters, aunts, uncles, grandfathers, grandmothers and cousins – a group of relations like any other family, which shares both joy and sorrow.

The same courtier who said he liked working with the family also said: "The great thing above all, though, is that they are such a nice family to be with". His view, fortunately, is still shared by millions of people throughout Britain and the Commonwealth. Despite the odd sniping from some quarters, the Royal Family is as popular as ever. The Queen must be one of the best-loved monarchs in the history of the British Crown.

She and those close to her, particularly the heir to the throne, Prince Charles, have been worried about how the "family firm" was prospering among the people in the streets. Any doubts they might have had were quelled by the cheers and enthusiasm shown for the monarchy during the Silver Jubilee celebrations of 1977.

The Queen was heartened by the spontaneous welcome she was given world-wide during that unforgettable year. Prince Charles was particularly encouraged to see that the bulk of the crowds was young people, many of them long-haired teenagers in tatty jeans – his future subjects. Among the banners being waved during the royal walkabout in London on Jubilee Day was a soccer-style placard: "Liz Rules–OK?".

She rules, in fact, by the rights of a constitution that goes back eleven centuries. The monarchy is the oldest secular institution in Britain, tracing its origins to 829; that was the year the Saxon King Egbert united England when he became King of Wessex and All England. The Queen traces her descent from Egbert, who reigned for twelve years.

According to some genealogists, the Royal Family can also claim in its ancestry the Prophet of Islam, Mohammed, and the first President of the United States, George Washington. As well as being related to almost every past and present royal family in Europe for over 150 years – thanks to the prolific breeding of Queen Victoria – The Queen and her children also include a few ordinary Smiths and Browns in their backgrounds.

Until the First World War the family belonged to the House of Saxe-Coburg and Gotha, a link with Queen Victoria's prince consort who was Prince Albert of Saxe-Coburg and Gotha. Feelings were running so high against Germany during the war that King George V made a proclamation in 1917 that Windsor would be the family name of all Queen Victoria's male descendants and in April 1952, before her coronation, Queen Elizabeth II declared that she and all her children should be known as the House and Family of Windsor.

The monarchy is four centuries older than Parliament and three centuries older than the British judicial system. Its continuity has been broken only once – that was the eleven years from 1649 to 1660, when Britain was governed by Oliver Cromwell.

Up to the end of the seventeenth century, when Parliament established a monarchy with limited rights, Queen Elizabeth's predecessors personally exercised supreme executive, legislative and judicial powers. By the end of the last century all the sovereign's political power was terminated and the Queen must now accede to Parliament's wishes and be an impartial head of State.

Although there are a number of Acts, as well as common law rules of descent, giving her the right to rule, the Queen stays on the throne essentially by the consent of her people. If the majority of her subjects turned against both her and the monarchial system, there could be pressure through Parliament to end the Windsor dynasty: a prospect that seems highly unlikely in an era when the British Royal Family is the strongest and most popularly supported of any of the monarchies which remain in a world of republicanism.

The Queen was never destined for the throne from birth. Her father and mother were the Duke and Duchess of York, and it was never thought likely that they would become King George VI and Queen Elizabeth. Her uncle, the popular Prince of Wales, was destined to succeed to the throne. That he would abdicate to marry the woman he loved was a dramatic gesture never imagined by the family of the uncrowned King Edward VIII.

Elizabeth, therefore, never anticipated being trained for the life of a monarch. She was "Lilibet", a cheerful child, not too serious, enjoying a privileged existence in a smart Mayfair house, outdoor fun at Royal Lodge, Windsor, and playing among the heather at Birkhall near Balmoral.

All this changed for her and her sister Margaret when they were ten and six years old respectively. Their uncle David gave up his throne and their father had to step into his shoes. From then on life took on a more serious aspect because now Elizabeth had to be trained to become a sovereign. Private lessons became more purposeful and a little of her lightheartedness disappeared as she became more involved in protocol and learning about the affairs of State. Until then she and Princess Margaret had grown up in a blissfully happy home, without any of the pressures of impending responsibility that, for example, Prince Charles has had to face.

Elizabeth spent her teenage years during the austerity of the Second World War, when she soon learned about the obligations of being a monarch as she shared the dangers of the Blitz in London with her father's subjects, and toured the war-torn areas of the country with her parents. When she was old enough she joined the Army, wearing khaki as an officer in the Auxiliary Territorial Service, the predecessor of today's Women's Royal Army Corps.

Few people who meet the Queen when she is in silken and bejewelled finery realise that those well-manicured hands have suffered their fair share of broken nails, cuts and oily bruises while servicing lorries. The Sovereign can count among her many talents that of a trained motor mechanic, a skill she acquired during her Army days.

The Queen was only twenty-five when her father died in February 1952. He died while Princess Elizabeth and Prince Philip were in Kenya on the first leg of a royal tour of East Africa, Australia and New Zealand.

His death did not come as a surprise to the princess and the rest of the family. He had been ill for more than three years, a grim piece of information that had been kept quiet from his subjects and the world at large. In March 1949 he underwent an operation to improve the circulation in his right foot. Two years later, the Queen Mother and the two princesses had confirmation of their worst fears – King George, a heavy smoker, had a cancerous growth in his left lung.

Surgeons did their best and after an operation the King seemed to make a bright recovery. It was not to last. Less than a year later the illness took its toll. Few who were present or saw newsreel and newspaper photographs will forget the haggard expression on his face as he waved farewell to his eldest daughter and her husband at London Airport when they set off on their world tour. It was a harsh winter's day. He was so ill that he should not have ventured out – yet it almost seems as if he sensed it might be the last time he would see his "Lilibet".

A week later he was at the royal estate of Sandringham, enjoying one of his favourite sports – shooting pheasant. At the end of the day he had dinner with his queen, listened to radio reports of Princess Elizabeth's tour in Africa, then had a cup of cocoa while he read a magazine. He went to bed and died in his sleep from a coronary thrombosis. The King was found dead by one of the valets, who drew back the curtains, turned round to say "good morning" and faced a stilled body. At 56 years of age the man who had never sought the throne, yet became one of Britain's greatest loved monarchs, had gone.

"Long live the Queen" was the shout from town hall steps throughout the Commonwealth as the official announcement of his death was made. A new Elizabethan Age had begun, four hundred years after the previous magnificent period in British history during the reign of the first Queen Elizabeth.

Above the muddy pond where lion and zebra drink in the Aberdare Forest of Kenya there was no rejoicing for a new golden age. Princess Elizabeth was told that she was now Queen after she and the Prince had spent the night in the hotel on stilts which was known as 'Treetops'. A father had died and all his daughter wanted to do was to cry and mourn his passing, comforted by her husband. The harshness of the responsibility of her new role, however, became clear to her as the day progressed.

From Treetops they returned to a nearby royal hunting lodge at Sagana where they had been spending a few days' holiday. By the time they arrived newsagency reports were confirmed by official telegrams and messages from London that made clear where her duties now lay. They were couched in courtly politeness, but it was evident that she was not to suffer her grief in private like a member of any other family. She was now Elizabeth the Queen, and, as such, she must be seen to rule as soon as possible. The public needed evidence that the majesty of monarchy would continue. The new Queen Elizabeth II therefore, in the days before Concorde, made a tiring night and day flight back to England with Prince Philip.

All the Royal Family carry around with them while they are on tour, at home or overseas, a suitcase which they hope they will never have to open containing mourning clothes. Smartly tailored, they are included in the luggage ready to wear should they have to dash back to London on receiving the news of a royal or stateman's death. The proprieties of public death have to be observed and Elizabeth changed on the last leg of her flight into a long black coat and cockaded black hat from that neglected suitcase.

As if to signify the loneliness of her new role, she walked down the aircraft steps by herself – a shy, almost timorous young woman, who had left London only eight days earlier as a carefree wife, and now returned to face the task of being one of the most significant personalities of the twentieth century. Waiting to greet her at the bottom of the aircraft steps was her Prime Minister, Winston Churchill.

Elizabeth had always hoped that she would never have to take the throne so soon after her marriage. She and Philip had been married for four years and were just beginning to settle down to enjoy the marvellous experience of being a young couple with children. She had wanted to go through the experience of being the wife of a naval officer, a mother of two growing children, and build a home and family life, just like any other woman, before accepting the duties of the Crown.

The fact that she had to assume royal duties so early in life, depriving her of so much of the freedom that others in their twenties can expect, has influenced, to a certain degree, the Queen's attitude towards Prince Charles. She knows what it is like to have to bear so early the monarchial chains of office. For this reason she wishes that Charles should have the chance to marry, set up a home and lead an undisturbed domestic life before it is his turn to take over the throne.

Prince Charles frequently says that it could be as long as thirty or forty years before he becomes king, pointing out how healthy and keen for the job his mother still is. Waiting for so long would mean Charles reaching his sixties before he has the chance to rule. The Queen and her advisers would, nevertheless, like the heir to the throne to still be young and full of vigour when his time to don the kingly mantle arrives. Should the Queen, as some people say, decide to abdicate in favour of her son, it will certainly not be until he has had a better chance than she had of being just a parent first and a monarch second.

Her full duties began in earnest sixteen months after her return to England as Queen, when Elizabeth was crowned in Westminster Abbey on a rainy June 2, 1953. The country, which was beginning to recover from the Second World War, still had the wealth and might of a major power and the coronation gave Britain the opportunity to demonstrate her imperial vigour to the world.

More than ten thousand servicemen – a quarter of them "soldiers of the Queen" from the Commonwealth – marched in the coronation procession. Two thousand bandsmen, making up nearly fifty bands, provided the music. Fellow sovereigns and rulers from all over the globe came to pay tribute to the girlish figure who was now the head of the greatest group of nations in history. A hundred thousand people braved the wet weather along the streets. Such was the length of the procession that it took 45 minutes to pass any one spot.

On the morning of the coronation there had been ructions at Buckingham Palace, because four-year old Charles was allowed to attend the ceremony while his sister, two years younger, was told that she would have to stay at home. There were tantrums, but the Queen insisted that Anne was too young to go to Westminster Abbey. As it turned out, the four-hour long service proved too much for the satin-suited Charles, anyway. He watched the crowning standing alongside his grandmother, but then he became impatient and noisy, so he and the Queen Mother left early.

When the Queen and Prince Philip returned to the palace they were hugged and kissed by the children, who were greeting their "mum and dad" – not a newly invested sovereign and her consort. Princess Anne, wearing a pretty white party frock was allowed to take part – at last – in some of the day's excitement. She and Charles came onto the balcony to wave to the crowds and see the fly-past by the Royal Air Force.

The family of Elizabeth and Philip had become truly royal. They were under great pressure in a changing world and faced public curiosity even into their most private moments.

In the years since her coronation the demands on the Queen have been enormous. With jet aircraft speeding up global travel, she, together with Prince Philip, has undertaken more tours abroad than any previous monarch. She has had to maintain stately calm and continuity during a period of industrial, social and political change. She has had to ensure the smooth transition of a colonial empire into a Commonwealth and yet, despite this hectic life, she has achieved a happy family existence with her husband and children.

The Queen's day when she is at Buckingham Palace usually begins with a call at eight every weekday morning. At around eight-thirty she joins Prince Philip and the rest of the family – if they are at home – in a first floor breakfast room overlooking the gardens and lake at the back of the building.

Morning newspapers are read during breakfast, with shared laughter if one of the family spots something written about them that appears to be distinctly outrageous. The first paper the Queen turns to is The Sporting Life – the horse-racing fraternity's "bible". Such is her enthusiasm for what has been called the "sport of kings" that the publishers send a copy by messenger straight from the presses each night.

The Queen, Prince Philip and now Prince Charles have an enormous amount of paperwork to deal with each day. No matter where they are in the world, dispatch boxes carrying Parliamentary or diplomatic documents, State briefings, letters – official and unofficial – and statements of household accounts arrive daily. In London the official papers reach Buckingham Palace during the night and early morning by car or horse-drawn carriage from Whitehall. When the family is abroad they are flown out, no matter whereabouts in the world they are staying.

Among the official letters the Queen has to deal with daily there is always a large batch of personal letters from friends – or warm, usually hand-written, greetings from just ordinary people all over the world.

Every letter is answered, and those sent out from Buckingham Palace are typed on special thick paper called "Original Turkey Mill Kent". They are easily recognised as they pop through postboxes because the envelopes bear no stamps; instead they are marked with E.R., the royal insignia, on front and back. Such is the amount of mail handled at the palace each day that it has its own post office, which is tucked away in the left-hand corner as one looks at the building from The Mall.

A staff of secretaries jets around the globe with the royal family. They tend to be very hard-working and not especially well paid: dictating letters, making phone calls or hammering away at typewriters more for the enjoyment and privileges of the job rather than for healthy bank accounts.

On overseas tours I have seen them trying to create

organisation out of chaos, setting up temporary offices in hotel rooms, or back rooms of palaces as they dash from city to city, country to country. Very often the most they see of their "boss" or the country they are visiting is by a quick glance at local television between handling correspondence, and arranging official functions.

The Queen appreciates the strenuous help she gets from her staff, so she usually says "thank–you" with a private dinner party on the last evening of a tour. The next morning they are busy again bundling type-writers, dictating machines, notepaper, files and other office paraphernalia into cases for yet another mad dash to one more airport.

In London the Queen's business day follows the pattern of Prince Philip and Prince Charles – except that she has more work to deal with. Her private secretary, Sir Philip Moore, is usually the first person to greet her in her study after breakfast. He will already have sorted out the more urgent documents and letters that need dealing with and they will discuss the schedule for the day. It would be a rare day when she had no official function in the palace, such as an investiture, or engagements somewhere in the country.

Dealing with correspondence and "the boxes", as the Cabinet and State papers are called, has to be fitted in between these appointments. As much work as possible is done in the morning, but Her Majesty often has to return to paperwork, which sometimes takes her late into the night, after she has shaken the last hand of the day and given a final wave to the crowds.

Documents in the dispatch boxes come mainly from the Prime Minister, the Foreign Secretary, Home Secretary and Commonwealth governments… she is, after all, not just the Queen of England. These papers either inform her of government proposals, fill in the background of events at home and abroad, or seek her signature on legislation. It might be a major bill or a minor reform overseas, but it still needs her signature under the constitution of Britain and the Commonwealth.

The Queen must be informed and consulted on every aspect of national life to the widest possible extent. She is also free to put forward her own views in private for the consideration of her ministers, but the final decision is always that of Parliament. That eminent Victorian, Walter Bagehot, described the sovereign as one who had "the right to be consulted, the right to encourage and the right to warn".

She does not merely rubber-stamp a document. She likes to be well briefed about current events, and although she has no power to alter the decisions of her various parliaments, she insists on knowing exactly to what she is putting her signature. Current parliamentary activities in Britain are discussed at the regular weekly meeting with the Prime Minister.

Her Majesty's advice and reaction to parliamentary affairs is frequently sought because of her vast political knowledge. Up to the time of the Silver Jubilee celebrations she had been served by seven prime ministers: five Conservatives and two Socialists. Her involvement in State affairs has been so rich and varied that Prince Charles has paid tribute to his mother as a repository of vast constitutional and political knowledge.

If she has no official engagements at mid-day the Queen helps herself to a light meal served buffet style. Hopefully she would have her husband or one of her children with her to share a relaxing lunch.

As part of the recent efforts by most of the royals to understand at first hand what is happening beyond the palace gates, the Queen now holds monthly lunches for about twelve people. Her guest list is deliberately wide, ranging from pop singers and comedians to ambassadors and visiting statesmen. They have proved to be highly successful, with both Sovereign and subjects getting to know each other better in a semi-formal atmosphere. One lucky guest recalls: "She goes out of her way to make you feel at ease, and by the time you've reached the second course you tend to forget that you are in the palace and begin to let your hair down…not too far down though".

One can never really let one's hair down in the presence of the Queen. No matter how friendly she may appear to be, due to her natural politeness and genuine interest in people, she may never forget who she is and what she represents. Over-familiarity is, therefore, stylishly put down. The Royal Family generally counts among its intimates three types of people – relations, overseas regal families, and long-standing friends. With these an informal pattern of banter is permitted. With others, however, politicians, visiting statesmen, guests at Buckingham Palace, staff and those fortunate enough to be in a line-up for a smile and handshake, conversation can go so far… then a degree of aloofness may be necessary. I doubt that any group of people in the world can use the affirmative "Yes" so effectively as they drawl it out and turn away from someone being either excruciatingly boorish or far too forward. "Yeees" and a quick move in another direction can be taken as a definite royal cut!

Prince Charles once employed a more exhausting response to a group of local politicians who were trying to give the impression that THEY had a special relationship with HIM at an agricultural show in Australia. Super-fit, commando–trained Charles shortened his stay with them by dashing round the grounds at a breakneck pace, leaving a trail of perspiring politicos behind him.

When someone is introduced to the Queen they are briefed beforehand to call her "Ma'am". Etiquette is such that one never takes her hand unless it is offered and then the grip must not be too strong–neither must it be too weak. She has a distaste for 'wet-fish' handshakes.

If the guest or nervous participant in a formal line-up has reached the stage of conversation then it too must be properly orchestrated. No one talks to the Queen…she always begins a discussion. People meeting her are warned beforehand that they must not let a brief chat develop into a monologue. This is because her time is usually short so she values a few words with everyone rather than being engaged in chit-chat with just one forceful acquaintance.

When she does stop to have a discussion with someone the person is often astonished at how much she knows about him or his interests. This is because she is very well served by her staff, who give her a detailed briefing on whom she is likely to meet. All the members of the family carrying out public duties receive this service, which, thanks to their training and excellent memories, creates exactly the right impression.

Speeches for the Queen and Prince Philip are generally researched and written by their staffs, after which they give final approval, and perhaps a few alterations. Princess Anne also has her speeches written for her, but Prince Charles always writes his own. In either case, whether it be one of the senior members of "the firm" or the junior directors, great care is taken to avoid controversy: a policy that might result in a speech without much sparkle, but at least it avoids political fireworks.

This is an impossible task at times, due to the forceful characters of both Prince Philip and Prince Charles. They have minds of their own: convictions regarding social and national responsibility, and they occasionally push through their own views... prepared to stand by what they say. Because of this, Philip more than Charles, has found himself in hot water, but he has declared that he honestly felt that what was stated needed to be made clear, no matter how unpopular it might be with some sections of the community.

On the lighter side of speech-making, copies of an address – prepared in special large-charactered type-writers – usually include in brackets the note "pause for laughter". The widely spaced sheets are read on the eve of delivery – in Charles' case with a glass of milk in his hands as a nightcap.

Evenings at home when there is no need to entertain or prepare for the next day, are often spent watching television. The Queen and all her family like comedy shows and pick up as many of the current TV catch-phrases as any other households. Prince Charles and Prince Andrew have a taste for zany idioms and tend to use them more than the other royals when they are with their friends.

Prince Philip is five years older than his wife. They are third cousins and great-great grandchildren of Queen Victoria. They met when, through his links with his uncle, Earl Mountbatten, he used to go to Windsor Castle during the Second World War when Philip was a young naval officer. Elizabeth was only sixteen at the time, and developed a typical teenage crush on the dashing young naval officer.

Philip was born a member of both the Greek and the Danish royal families, the only son of Prince Andrew of Greece and Princess Alice of Battenberg.

His parents were not entirely happy together and, as a result, he and his mother spent most of his childhood from the age of eight, in England with relatives. Philip was educated in Britain and eventually followed the footsteps of Earl Mountbatten and joined the Royal Navy.

After graduating from Dartmouth Naval College, just before the outbreak of the war, he went to sea as a second lieutenant. Two years later he faced his first blooding in action on board a battleship against the Italian fleet off Cape Matapan. As a regard for his courageous and cool behaviour under fire he was mentioned in despatches. He was serving on the battleship HMS Valiant at the time and right in the midst of fierce shell fire was manning a searchlight. His Captain said of him: "Thanks to his alertness and appreciation of the situation we were able to sink in five minutes two eight-inch gun Italian cruisers".

Much to the distress of the young Princess Elizabeth he was not a popular choice with her parents. At first King George and Queen Elizabeth thought their elder daughter should meet other young men before deciding on a husband.

Philip's nationality, too, was a problem; he was a Greek national although he was trying to become a naturalised Briton. In addition his four sisters had all married into German aristocracy – unions that did not go down well in Britain at that time.

It was not until two years after the war was over that he was able to gain naturalisation papers and become a British subject – Philip Mountbatten. A few days after hearing this news the King told an ecstatic Elizabeth that she could marry her sailor. The wedding brought the first post-war cheer to a glum world in 1947.

Their first child was born a year after their marriage, on a gloomy Sunday evening at the end of November 1948. Instead of pacing up and down a hospital corridor for hours in the classic manner of an expectant father, Prince Philip sweated away a few hours with some hectic games of squash.

The circumstances of the birth of Prince Charles at Buckingham Palace represented a break from tradition. For centuries it was the custom for a cabinet minister to be present at the delivery of an heir to the throne – to make sure there was no bedchamber jiggery-pokery and that a substitute child was not smuggled in by bedwarmer perhaps! Elizabeth was the first royal mother to produce a direct heir who did not have to suffer this embarrassment.

Queen Victoria is reputed to have been as imperious as ever, having just gone through the pains of childbirth, when dealing with a representative of government on one occaision. The frock-coated gentleman said to the queen: "You have given birth to a fine healthy boy, your majesty". The unruffled monarch responded regally from her bed: "Prince you mean minister ... prince!"

Charles' great-grandfather, George V, once said: "My father was frightened of his father ... I was frightened of my father ... and I'm going to see to it that my children are frightened of me."

Palace views on dealing with offspring are, happily, more enlightened today than the early days of this century when this Victorian–Edwardian attitude prevailed.

Charles and Philip have a very close relationship, though their personalities differ. Prince Philip is slightly aggressive, while his eldest son is more gentle of character. Friends of both of them have said, for example, that Charles will never match his father's achievements on the polo field because he is too kind to his horses.

Both father and son tend to have the same mannerisms: the same briskness of walk, that well-known habit of clenching their hands behind their backs, thrusting a left hand in the jacket pocket, and flinging their heads back when laughing. Charles once explained why they have the habit of holding their hands behind their backs: "We both use the same tailor and he always makes the sleeves so tight that we can't get our hands in front."

All the royal sons seem to have inherited their father's sense of humour: a liking for zany, outrageous slapstick – the ludicrous rather than sharpness of wit.

The tastes of Charles and his father are generally, however, quite different. Charles enjoys music, whereas Prince Philip finds it agonizing to have to sit through a concert. Charles favours solitary pastimes, while Philip is much more gregarious.

Prince Philip had considerable influence in the upbringing of the heir to the throne, however. Up to the age of eight Charles spent his time with nannies and governesses. The Queen had been following the pattern of her own childhood – and the tradition of centuries – by giving Charles a private education within palace walls. Philip changed all this, not just for Charles, but for Anne, Andrew and Edward as well.

In Charles' case, Philip, realising the restrictions of such an education, sent him to school with boys of his generation to learn how to live with other children. Dancing lessons were stopped, music lessons took a few bars rest, and, instead, Charles was taken to a playing field in Chelsea, to get into the rough and tumble of soccer, and a private gymnasium twice a week for work-outs on climbing ropes, parallel bars and vaulting horses.

Charles was taught nearly all his physical skills by his father, and in this way they grew closer to each other. Philip took him out in bitter wintry weather to teach him to shoot among the heather around Balmoral, and Charles shot his first grouse when he was ten years old. Philip taught his son how to fish, and when he was at home he would spend an hour after tea teaching his son to swim in the pool at the palace. Charles could swim a length before he was five years old, and is now an excellent swimmer.

Father and son would occasionally have a boisterous game of football in the palace grounds, with the corgis barking round their heels. The Queen and toddler Anne might be permitted to join in the fun now and again.

The Prince was determined that his son would not have a pampered, soft life. He once noticed a servant leaping to close a door that schoolboy Charles had failed to shut. He shouted: "Leave it alone, man. He's got hands. He can go back and do it himself."

Prince Philip's greatest influence in the early days was in bringing the royal educational style into the twentieth century. He made sure that the boys learnt independence as soon as possible, packing them off to boarding schools where they had to stand on their own two feet from the age of nine or ten years old. Anne, too, left the shelter of home at thirteen to become a boarder at the fashionable Benenden School in Kent.

The boys, at their father's instigation, were to face a tougher educational regime when they reached thirteen. Philip sent them to his old alma-mater, Gordonstoun, on a bleak stretch of Scotland's west coast. He had been subjected to its harsh, cold-shower system and had thought it had done him the world of good. Why wouldn't it have the same results with his own sons?

Gordonstoun was to be an institution that Andrew – who has inherited his father's ways – found easier to accept. Charles and Edward are more sensitive than the middle brother. Charles has especially unhappy memories of Gordonstoun, which was founded by the late Dr Kurt Hahn, who developed his tough educational philosophy originally in Germany to educate the sons of a Junkers-style aristocracy.

The school is mainly a collection of crude huts. Dormitories have unpainted wooden walls, bare floors, and uncomfortable iron beds. An obligatory cold shower has to be taken every morning, no matter what the weather. The school motto, "Plus est en vous" ("There is more in you"), heralds a harsh system aimed at stretching to the fullest both physical and intellectual capabilities.

Charles was certainly not given preferential treatment; his housemaster gave him an unsavoury task in his first term – emptying the dustbins each day. After Charles left Gordonstoun he said: "I did not enjoy school as much as I might have, but that was because I am happier at home than anywhere else".

All the royal sons and daughter are great home lovers. As a group they are closer to each other and their near relations than most other families these days. Their happiest moments are when they are together. Whether at Buckingham Palace or one of the other royal homes, they are a tight little group that finds a welcome relief from the pressures around them. When the cheers and flagwaving have ended, they still have each other.

They value one another, and protect one another. If any of them are abroad they keep in constant touch by telephone or letter. None of them does anything without discussing it first with the others.

During the tragedy of the break-up of her marriage, Princess Margaret was helped through the experience by her family. The Queen and Prince Philip took a sympathetic interest in what was happening not merely because of a constitutional responsibility, but because they wished to offer filial comfort.

Their concern was also extended to Lord Snowdon and the couple's children, Viscount Linley and Sarah Armstrong-Jones. Lord Snowdon is still in close touch with the family at the end of The Mall and with the Queen Mother, despite the divorce.

The Queen best summed up her attitude towards family life when she said at the time of her silver wedding anniversary: "A marriage begins by joining man and wife together, but this relationship between two people, however deep at the time, needs to develop and mature with the passing years. For that it must be held firm in the web of the family relationships, between parents and children, between grandparents and grandchildren, between cousins, aunts and uncles. If I am asked today what I think about family life after 25 years of marriage I can answer with simplicity and conviction. I am for it."

The cost to the taxpayers of the Royal Family is around £5,000,000 a year. Two million pounds goes towards the upkeep of royal residences and paying for travel – including the cost of the small fleet of aircraft belonging to the Queen's Flight of the Royal Air Force. Nearly £2,600,000 is paid to members of the family through the Civil List, Parliament's "pay cheque" for The Queen and her close relatives.

Individual payments include: The Queen – £1,950,000; the Queen Mother – £175,000; Duke of Edinburgh – £93,500; Princess Margaret – £59,000; Princess Anne – £60,000; Prince Andrew – £17,262 (kept in trust); Princess Alice of Gloucester – £30,000; Duke of Gloucester – £39,000; Duke of Kent – £60,000; Princess Alexandra – £60,000; and Princess Alice of Athlone – £6,500.

Charles has no State salary so he takes on other tasks to raise enough money to carry out his official duties. He heads an organisation which administers his Duchy of Cornwall estates. The average annual net profits are £220,000. Half of this is given to the nation while Charles retains £110,000 – tax free. It has been estimated that on current rates of taxation he would have to actually earn a gross of well over a million pounds a year to be able to put that net figure in the bank.

The total area of the Duchy is 130,000 acres, which makes Charles one of the biggest landowners in Britain. It is a mixture of farms and country homesteads, old terraced houses, shops and even pubs, spreading west from London.

Outside London his tenants include sheep farmers on Dartmoor, Cornish tin miners, and daffodil growers in the Scillies. In Cornwall he has an oyster farm which produces a million tasty morsels every year.

It is often mistakenly thought that the money which goes to the Queen and her relations is just spending money; income to be frittered away on caviar and fast cars. This money is, in fact, used to pay their staffs and cover the costs of official duties. Whenever the Royal Family has a pay rise, this is to meet the increases in costs of living of their staffs.

The line of succession to the throne is: Prince Charles; Prince Andrew; Prince Edward; Princess Anne; her son Master Peter Phillips; Princess Margaret; her son Viscount Linley and daughter, Lady Sarah Armstrong-Jones; The Queen's cousin, the Duke of Gloucester; his son the Earl of Ulster and daughter, Lady Davina Windsor; the Queen's cousin, the Duke of Kent; his elder son, the Earl of St. Andrews; his younger son, Lord Nicholas Windsor and his daughter, Lady Helen Windsor; the Queen's cousin and sister of the Duke of Kent, Princess Alexandra; her son, James Ogilvy and daughter, Marina Ogilvy.

The Royal Family exists at a time of changing attitudes towards monarchies everywhere. They realise well enough that the days of an aloof monarch on a golden throne are over. The continuance of their very being is now questioned in the Houses of Parliament.

With this in mind, they have tried over the past 25 years to become close to the people. They seek to know how people live and cope with the problems of our pressurised society: how people exist in small houses or rented flats and cope on meagre salaries. Charles, above all, constantly wishes to meet as many people as possible from all walks of life, to exchange ideas, and to learn how others hope to fulfil their lives. He once said: "I am not a normal person in the sense that I was born to be king. I have received a special education and training. I could never be a normal person because I have been prepared to reign over my subjects".

Amid all the demands on her time as Sovereign, Elizabeth has always managed to fulfil what to her is still the most important role in her life – being a wife and mother. She has helped her children through all the usual growing pains of youth and those moments of bewilderment with life. Her encouragement is always there whenever one of them thinks the going is getting too tough. Princess Anne, now a mother herself and setting up her new home and way of life with her husband, Mark, and son, Peter, can still turn to her parents for help and advice.

Elizabeth remembered the warm, loving atmosphere of her own childhood so she arranged that there would be no barriers of governesses and nannies between herself and her own children. Nursery staff were employed – but mother and father were the people the children usually saw first thing in the morning and last thing at night.

As toddlers the children would snuggle up alongside their mother to look at a picture book, or to listen to a story. They were all capable of pranks and mischief, however. Charles used to race round the corridors of Buckingham Palace with his friends, play risky games of hide and seek on the roof of Windsor Castle, or slip a piece of ice down the collar of a footman. When they deserved it, they would get a good spanking, particularly if they were rude to servants. The Queen and Prince Philip viewed such things very seriously because their victims could never answer back.

To teach them the value of money, pocket money has been given in small amounts. Although Prince Andrew is now entitled to an income of more than £17,000 a year, the Queen insisted that the 18-year-old should not be handed this amount. It is being kept in trust for him and he is given a small allowance each week.

At home Elizabeth and Philip are just ordinary parents to their children – a mother and father they can turn to for advice and help. When any of the Royal Family refers to the Queen in public, however, it is always on a very formal basis. She is never called "my mother" in a speech…always "the Queen", although Prince Philip is frequently called "my father".

Charles has said of his father's influence on his education: "His attitude was very simple. He told me what were the pros and cons. Of all the possibilities and attractions he told me what he thought best. Because I had come to see how wise he was, by the time I had to be educated I had perfect confidence in my father's judgement. When children are young you have decide for them. How can they decide for themselves?"

It was his father's influence, above all others, that persuaded Charles to choose a career in the Royal Navy. Philip always felt that Charles should have a service career and the best training, as far as Prince Philip was concerned, was in his own beloved Navy. The reason? "It has several advantages as a training ground" explained Philip, "You learn to live with people of all sorts. You have to develop a professional ability. Aboard ship you learn to live with people, and this is the most important thing."

The closeness of this remarkable family unit has given the royal children the confidence to venture into the world.

The Queen takes a special interest in the youngest of the family, 14-year-old Edward, who is the last to leave home and is now having to cope with the tough life of Gordonstoun. In between dealing with that huge daily official mail bag, she sends him letters regularly, passing on family gossip and words of encouragement. To help him through his schooldays she is trying to keep him out of the limelight – letting him cope with the business of growing up without the problems of publicity.

Throughout the childhood of all of her offspring there were always requests for the young princess and princes to appear in public. The Queen resisted them all, no matter how worthy the cause asking for their presence. She remembered how, as a young princess, she was suddenly thrust into the public arena. She insisted that her youngsters should have a normal childhood, as far as this was possible. To her, they were above everything else, children; so the Queen protected them and carefully nurtured them to the stage when they could be made aware of their Stately duties.

All the youngsters, however, had to suffer an odd

aspect of upbringing, unique to royalty. As part of the training for a ceremonial life, they were taught to stand motionless for long periods to accustom them to the discomforts ahead. (The late Duke of Windsor when commenting on coping with the problem of endless standing in public once said that the best advice his father had ever given him about public appearances was to always take the weight off his feet whenever he could and to go to the toilet whenever possible!)

Making friends outside their own close circle is difficult for the royal children. They are very wary of becoming too close to people or making easy friendships because they suspect – correctly in some instances – that many are interested purely for social advantages or to gossip about them afterwards. As a result it is a privilege indeed to be counted as one of the palace "in people". This means that you have been vetted and found truly trustworthy as well as being an amusing and interesting companion.

The Royal Family have become reluctant to express any controversial views in public because, apart from sometimes causing too much of a stir, once recorded their remarks take on a permanency that can become embarrassing for the future. They avoid taking a stand on an issue. Views are often put forward as rhetorical questions rather than statements. The simplest remark can sometimes cause offence, as Prince Charles once discovered during a tree-planting ceremony in Wales when he said: "Thank goodness it's an oak and not one of those ghastly spruces". There were immediate letters of protest from hundreds of forestry workers who had devoted their lives to planting "ghastly spruces".

The Queen and Prince Charles have much in common. He shares her kindness and gentle qualities and, as neither of them like dramatic change, both have the same conservative attitudes. They are also aware of the continuing constitutional roles they shoulder. They sense that they not only belong to the nation and Commonwealth but are also the ongoing link of this tradition.

They are both frustrated actors, and often turn to mimicry to amuse the family and staff at the end of a day of being introduced to government officials or city fathers. They have a cruel ability to impersonate the more pompous of those they have met. A remarkable number of politicians or captains of industry would curb their tales of passing acquaintance with the royals if they could see the palace "cabaret" later.

The Queen, Prince Philip and their children are all keen on horse-riding, but Her Majesty has an out of the ordinary interest in the sport. Her main hobby is both breeding and racing horses, and her enthusiasm almost borders on an obsession.

Her enthusiasm for equine activities began as a child when she used to share her father's joy as his string of racehorses frequently won their races. When he died she inherited not only his two studs in Norfolk, but also his spirit for the sport. The story goes that on the eve of her coronation a lady-in-waiting said to her: "You must be feeling apprehensive Ma'am" and the Queen is said to have replied: "Yes, but I'm sure my horse will still win". Her horse was Aureole, a worthy animal that came second in the Derby a few days after her crowning. She has four stables where she breeds and trains, keeping a close eye on her studs.

In addition to the breeding she has twenty to thirty thoroughbreds in training, which between them usually bring in a fair amount of money each year. Such is her skill as an expert on pedigrees that over the last twenty-five years she is estimated to have won more than a million pounds in prize money.

Exactly when Philip first met the Queen varies from biographer to biographer, friend to friend. They certainly started to fall in love with each other at their meetings during the war, when the young princess noticed him as a possible suitor, but there were earlier meetings which were of no romantic significance at the time.

According to Miss Marion Crawford – the famous "Crawfie" – who was governess to Princess Elizabeth and Princess Margaret from 1932 to 1949, they met at the beginning of 1939. At this time Elizabeth and Margaret went with their father to visit Dartmouth Royal Naval College. Thirteen-year-old Elizabeth, at the age when she was beginning to take an interest in boys, was impressed by the tennis prowess of the blonde nephew of Earl Mountbatten. Philip was eighteen at the time and had just begun his training at Dartmouth. To him the two princesses were just little girls who had to be entertained and he is said not to have made much of a fuss over them.

As we know, King George VI was not keen, at first, on his "Lilibet" being involved so early in life with Philip when she was in her late teens, but he clearly changed his attitude after their wedding when he wrote to Elizabeth: "I can see that you are sublimely happy with Philip."

Marrying Princess Elizabeth brought Philip a stable family life for the first time. Until then he had been virtually a nomad, from a royal line exiled from its throne in Greece, a child living with relatives throughout Europe after the break-up of his parents' marriage, and a solitary naval officer who had never really known a permanent home.

His mother, Princess Alice of Battenburg, was a sister of Earl Mountbatten and a member of the British royal family. A brave woman, she stayed in Athens during the German occupation helping Jewish refugees escape from the Gestapo. In 1949 she founded a reclusive order of nuns, the Christian Sisterhood of Martha and Mary, then led a humble existence with them until her death in 1969.

Philip is a man of great integrity – someone who has been used to standing alone and fighting for himself – without expecting favouritism of any sort. One aspect of this side of his character emerged during the early days of his marriage.

Princes Elizabeth had joined him in Malta to share, as near as possible, the ways of a naval officer's wife. It was during the days when the British Mediterranean Fleet still filled Valetta harbour, and Philip was one of hundreds of young officers belonging to a force that continued to prove that Britannia ruled the waves. He might be the husband of a future queen, but he was also a navy man devoted to his career. The possibility of standing on the left-hand side of a sovereign seemed remote.

Like all budding Nelsons or Drakes he had occasionally to take examinations in his chosen profession to further his chances of promotion. While Elizabeth was in Malta with him he failed a course in anti-submarine warfare by a narrow margin. It was suggested that because the marks were so marginal he should be allowed through. When

Philip heard about this suggestion he refused such an easy passage and insisted on taking the examinations again. He did, and passed with flying colours!

Philip achieved his ambition of being given a ship of his own in 1950, when he was thirty years old. His days as skipper of the frigate H.M.S. Magpie were short lived, however, because the illness of George VI was becoming painfully evident. The queen-to-be and her husband had to start preparing for the duties that were inevitably so near.

After less than a year with his own ship, Lieutenant-Commander Philip Mountbatten left the sea in June 1951 to join his wife and family in Britain and to take part in State duties. He was given what the navy called "extended leave" – a military status he still lives under today, though now he is an Admiral of the Fleet.

After the coronation he could have stayed at home and lived off his wife's prestige and income, but instead he set out from the beginning to do something useful for the community. He became involved with promoting British industry and exports and he introduced the Duke of Edinburgh Award Scheme to encourage young people to excel in endeavours ranging from mountain climbing to playing music and writing poetry. Above all, he became a drum beater for Britain and the Commonwealth, willing to fly anywhere to give a speech on behalf of the people and the group of nations he had fought for and adopted as his own.

Nothing seems too much trouble for a cause he might throw his weight and energy behind. When he was touring the United States raising money for the Variety Club of Great Britain, a pushy local businessman in Miami offered to hand over a cheque for 100,000 dollars if "the dook" would jump into his swimming pool. Philip stripped off, dived in, and collected the money.

One of the first ways in which Philip impressed the public was with his geniality. The Queen had been reluctant, at first, to go around with what is now a familiar happy face, because she thought her office was such that she should try to maintain dignity and solemnity. Philip always had a ready laugh, a quick joke, and a generally pleasant demeanour as he went about his public business. How could anyone fail to like a man with such an obvious sense of well-being?

Over the past 20 years he has become a royal personage entirely of his own making, more than someone in the shadow of the Crown; a man of importance in his own right. Yet he never forgets in public that it is the Queen, above all, who matters. He goes out of his way when they are together to draw attention to her.

A strong-willed husband and father he may be at Buckingham Palace, but in public he goes to great lengths to make it clear to those watching that he is the consort – and nothing more – to the Queen while on official duties.

The great affection they have for each other is clear in public. When the Queen is obviously enjoying herself she always glances across to her husband to signal her pleasure. Somehow, he always manages to have turned his head in her direction at the very same moment.

Prince Philip has a charming manner with his wife. It is a delightful mixture of obeisance to her as the monarch combined with that of a fond husband. He stays a step or two behind her as they walk along, allowing her to set the pace. He never attempts to upstage her; a difficult task for any husband to

perform, and, one imagines, on onerous role for someone so forceful in his ways.

Yet always one notices that he seems, clearly, to be a strength to the Queen. If she has forgotten to follow the programme exactly and there might be some confusion, the prince has an unobtrusive way of reminding her about some oversight.

As they drive through the crowds it is usually Prince Philip who suggests that they might sit on the boot of an open car so that she can be seen to better advantage.

Together they make a well-matched, loving team.

Without doubt one of the most popular royal personalities is the Queen Mother, the world's favourite grandmother. She is now approaching her eighties, but is still very active and carries out her share of public duties. Wherever she goes she is greeted with warmth and affection, something she immediately responds to with that beautiful ready smile that brightens up the dullest day. She has always been the favourite among Press photographers because she invariably takes the trouble to pause well within the lens range and turns in their direction. In a presentation line-up she usually pauses to talk to someone about four persons from the end – a handy distance for the cameramen.

The Queen Mother has had to suffer much in her life, yet she remains cheerful. She was barely a queen before she and her husband had to cope with wartime leadership. They refused to leave London during the Blitz, insisting on sharing all the dangers of their subjects. She then had only a few years of a peaceful reign before George VI became ill. The older generation of staff at Buckingham Palace still remember how much of a comfort she was to her husband, keeping his spirits high despite his great pain.

Recently she had the sadness of seeing her youngest daughter's marriage break up. During this time she was not only a motherly solace to Princess Margaret, but also a loving "granny" to her children.

She never expected to be a queen, but proved to be one of the finest consorts a British king could ever have had.

The Queen Mother was born Elizabeth Bowes-Lyon, the fourth daughter of Lord and Lady Glamis of Glamis Castle in Angus, Scotland – which was the setting Shakespeare chose for Macbeth's murder of King Duncan.

By the time she made her debut at court at the age of nineteen, she was already beginning to turn the heads of London society as a beautiful, long dark-haired girl with fiery blue eyes.

Drawing room gossip of the time praised her as being irresistible to men, but the gamin-like young Bowes-Lyon soon took a liking to King George V's second son, the Duke of York. After spending one of several weekends at Glamis Castle with her, the 25-year-old duke told his mother: "The more I see Elizabeth the more I like her". He fell madly in love with her and she with him but it needed three years of wooing before Elizabeth agreed to marry him. She was wary of marrying a king's son because of the enormous responsibilites it could bring – fears that were to prove justified.

The first few years of kingship were far from easy, as George was ill-prepared for the enormous task that had suddenly been thrust upon him. He had a lot to cope with and Elizabeth was a marvellous helpmate, always available to cheer him up.

It was a period too, when, because of the abdication crisis, the future of the monarchy was in doubt. The new queen helped to restore affection towards the throne by making an attempt to go out and meet the people, setting the style that is now almost commonplace with the Royal Family.

When her eldest daughter was suddenly brought to the throne while she was so young, it was her mother, always in the background, who gave her encouragement and wise counsel and did what grannies do all over the world – looked after the children.

The greatest joy of the Queen Mother's later years has been her six grandchildren, and now her great-grandchild, Master Peter, son of Anne and Mark. She has always had a soft spot, however, for Charles, more than for any of the others. Apart from being her first grandchild, he also reminds her of her late husband with his gentle, kindly ways.

Charles spent many years of his early childhood with his grandmother during the time that the Queen and Prince Philip were on tours abroad. As he grew into his teens it was often the Queen Mother he would turn to for help in sorting out the confusion of growing up.

Today they are still very close to each other. When Charles wants to relax he frequently joins the Queen Mother at one of her Scottish retreats to go fishing with her. At this stage of her life the "Queen Mum" is a very happy and contented woman. She has seen her daughter become one of the most admired monarchs in history, she is surrounded by loving grandchildren and continues to be close to the hearts of millions of people throughout the world.

The heir to the throne is an amazing person, with immense personal courage. Apart from being a skilled frogman, he has skippered a ship, piloted helicopters, flown jet fighters, driven tanks, trained as a tough commando and as a parachutist. If all these were not enough he is also an excellent horseman and a top class polo player.

Charles has, however, a sensitive ear for music, plays the piano and cello, paints landscapes and holds a degree in archaeology and anthropology. Such is the sensitive side of the nature of this well-rounded man that he has also been known to say when he hears a piece of music by Berlioz: "I am so moved that I'm reduced to tears every time."

He has a tremendous thirst for danger and adventure. According to the Queen Mother: "If there was anything left to discover in the world Charles would have been an explorer".

Says the prince: "I like to see if I can challenge myself to do something that is potentially hazardous, just to see if I can mentally accept that challenge and carry it out. I like to try all sorts of things because they appeal to me. I'm one of those people who don't like sitting and watching someone else doing something. I don't like to go to the races to watch horses thundering up and down…I'd rather be riding the horses myself."

Charles, who gets his love for flying from his father, has flown twice-the-speed-of-sound Phantom fighter bombers, strategic nuclear bombers, and is a naval helicopter pilot trained to land Royal Marine commandos in combat conditions. He was twenty when he first flew solo in a single-engined propeller-driven Chipmunk. According to his instructor, he had an immediate aptitude for flying. Others who have accompanied him in the cockpits of many aircraft since then all agree that he is a "natural" airman. Does he find flying some of the exotic jet aircraft he has laid his hands on dangerous? "No, it's more dangerous crossing the road", says the daredevil prince.

Charles also picked up his enthusiasm for polo from his father. It is the one great passion they have in common. Philip had taken up the game shortly after his marriage so that he could share the Queen's enthusiasm for horses.

As a toddler Charles would watch Prince Philip play and throughout his early teens was constantly pestering his father to let him mount up and join him. Charles used to help around the stables or act as a sort of 'squire', holding the polo sticks or being ready with a bottle of water between chukkas. Philip thought he was too young to take part in a game until he was in his mid-teens, but until then he taught him how to handle a pony and the difficult knack of ball control. The pair of them would ride off into Windsor Great Park for practice sessions.

Charles is now a better rider than his father, but, as I mentioned earlier, experts say that he will never be able to match him as a polo player because, according to one of them: "Charles shows far too much consideration for his horses and will not drive them hard enough."

Charles began playing the game at sixteen and now keeps a string of ponies at Windsor – his biggest extravagance. He says: "I love the game, I love the ponies and I love the exercise. It's my favourite game." He has played all over the world, including India, from where the game was brought to Europe by the officers of the British Raj in the nineteenth century.

With the use of a ready sense of humour Charles probably tries harder than other members of his family at getting down to the grass-roots level. He has a genuine interest in people from all walks of life and feels that getting to know his future subjects is of vital importance.

The five years he spent in the Royal Navy was very useful to him in this respect. He not only met fellow officers from wealthy homes but also had to deal with the problems of seamen from quite humble homes. He was responsible for their welfare and that could include dealing with marriage problems or telling someone the sad news that a relative had died.

When he is about his official duties Charles likes as few barriers as possible between himself and the crowds – a security man's nightmare at times. He does not like people to be nervous about approaching him or regarding him as a distant, god-like creature. As he once said: "I used to think 'Good God what's wrong? Do I smell? Have I forgotten to change my socks?' I realize now that I have to make a bit of the running and show that I am a reasonable human being. An awful lot of people say eventually: 'Good Lord, you're not nearly as pompous as I thought you were going to be!'"

When will Charles take over the throne? There has been great speculation about this, ranging from five years hence to as much as forty years ahead. A frequently discussed theory is that the Queen will abdicate in his favour before he gets too old to bring all his youthful vigour with him to kingship.

When asked about his mother giving up the throne to make way for him, Charles has replied on two occasions that it could be as much as thirty years, or forty years, before he is crowned.

If the wait is going to be that long it could make him sixty or even well into his seventieth year before he sits on the throne. Yet the prince insists that he sees no reason why the Queen should retire. She is healthy and absolutely on top of the job she is doing.

Should Her Majesty, as happily seems likely, live to the great ages of her mother, grandmother (86) or great-great-grandmother, Queen Victoria (82) it could be the twenty-first century before Charles achieves his destiny.

(That colourful Paris weekly newspaper France Dimanche, has, by the way, reported the Queen's abdication at least seventy times as well as carrying more than eighty stories about her intention to divorce Prince Philip. The paper is regularly sent to Buckingham Palace by the British Embassy because the family consider it to be "amusing light reading".)

A previous Prince of Wales, Victoria's son King Edward VII, did not begin his reign until he was 58 years old, after a wasteful life trying to relieve the boredom of waiting. He was not allowed to take part in any of the affairs of State, so he turned to a profligate existence, setting a life style that gave his name to an era.

Queen Elizabeth is at least making sure that Charles has a useful role to play, training him for the future by involving him in official duties and ensuring that he does his share of royal tours.

Before Charles reaches his coronation, however, he will need to find a wife. Gossip columnists the world over have been providing him with suitable spouses since he was barely able to walk.

The prince told a woman's magazine in 1973 that he would probably get married when he was "around thirty". Now that he has reached that age it is generally assumed that he is about to walk down the aisle of Westminster Abbey with a bride.

No matter how long he waits for his throne he can never be accused of being a wastrel. He has a busy schedule every working day, involving touring about the world, promoting his own principality of Wales, and organising youth schemes or bringing the palace nearer to the people with his friendly walk-abouts.

The young prince, more perhaps than others in his family, is aware that he is waiting for kingship in a changing society. He has said: "In these times the monarchy is called into question – it is not taken for granted as it used to be. In that sense one has to be far more professional than I think one ever used to be." To him, however, it is keeping pace, adapting to the new conditions, maintaining the institution as one of the strongest elements in keeping stability in Britain. Opinion polls usually show that, next to the Queen, he is the most popular member of the Royal Family.

Most of the family seems to have established in people's minds that they are "horsey-types" – perhaps because the one hobby that they are most frequently participating in publicly is either at a race track or in or around a show ring or polo field. They are interested in horses, but not to the exclusion of other hobbies and interests. Every one of them has a liking for photography, for example – both still and movie. The Queen and Prince Philip often keep a cine film record of their tours abroad, and there is an amusing collection of still photographs showing Press photographers in their off-guarded moments – one way, I suppose, in which the family can get their own back on the media.

They are great home-movie buffs, constantly taking cine shots of each other, just like any other family. A get-together at Buckingham Palace often includes a film show, with the typical silly scenes that parents and children find privately amusing the world over. When they gather to see the latest production, though, they do not have to squeeze into the front room where "dad" has hung the screen from a wall. On the first floor of Buckingham Palace there is a large private cinema, the decor of which is unlike any other. The walls have red cloth paper and dotted about are polished cabinets containing collections of fine porcelain. The seats are painted gold.

In the "interval" between changing films the audience can pull back one of the plush curtains, open a french window and step onto a balcony giving them a view of the gardens. It is slightly different, is it not, from the average neighbourhood theatre? Charles likes making pictures which are slightly zany in their humour. While on a training exercise in Canada with his Royal Navy helicopter squadron he produced, directed and edited a movie in which he played "Bluebottle", the mentally subnormal midget of Goon Show fame, who was being bossed around by all the other officers in his group.

Acting is an interest of the Queen and Prince Charles. She used to perform in pantomimes at Windsor as a child – she was once Prince Charming to Princess Margaret's Cinderella – while Charles has acted in public on a few occasions when he took part in student reviews during his days at Cambridge University. In one of them he sat on stage as a target for custard pies, and in another sketch he walked on under an umbrella with the remark: "I lead a very sheltered life you know!"

Acting has now, however, to be limited to family charades. On one occasion the Queen led the rest of the family to the opening of a cottage Lord Snowdon had just bought. The Queen Mother cut a ribbon across the door in her well-established "official opening" manner, while the rest of the family played the parts of applauding gawpers.

Prince Philip, Prince Charles and the Queen Mother all enjoy fishing. They cast for salmon and trout, usually when they are on holiday at Balmoral. Charles is considered such an expert on fly fishing that he has been able to write knowledgeably about it.

Most of the family have tried their hands at painting, but Charles, Andrew and their father have proved to be the most adept in this field, Philip being particularly sensitive with oils.

With a rugged, outdoor father to show the way it is not surprising that all the boys, and Anne, are keen on sport. Charles, as we know, is a skilled polo player, but lately he has taken up the craze of cross-country team eventing. This is a hairy weekend pastime in which groups of four riders charge across a local hunt course in competition with other teams. It has tremendous neck-breaking possibilities, a perfect challenge for Charles, who frequently falls off, brushes himself down, remounts and gallops off again.

Allthough he goes cross-country team eventing with hunts, he does not share Princess Anne's consuming interest in fox hunting. Charles has turned out now and again, though, resplendent in topper, cravat and blue riding coat with gold lapels, a riding habit that would make Beau Brummel envious.

Andrew shows all the signs of taking after his older brother as a daredevil. He is keen on football, rugby and ice-hockey, and has the same desire to fly. He won his glider pilot's wings while serving with Gordonstoun's Air Training Corps and he is about to begin flying training that will eventually take him up to jet-fighter standards.

Edward shows a keenness for football, rugby and cricket and he has started to go sailing with Andrew in the waters around Gordonstoun.

Although Andrew and Edward have taken up sailing, one of their father's favourite hobbies, Charles never developed the same enthusiasm for it as Prince Philip. Neither do they seem to follow the same tack when they are afloat, as Charles once recalled: "I remember one disastrous day when we were racing and my father, as usual, was shouting. We wound the winch harder and the sail split in half with a sickening crack; father was not pleased! Not long after that I was banned from the boat after an incident cruising off Scotland. There was no wind and I was amusing myself taking pot shots at beer cans floating around the boat. The only gust of wind that day blew the jib in front of my rifle just as I fired. I wasn't invited back on board...."

Prince Charles and Prince Philip do, however, both enjoy shooting. Charles is keen on the gun and his standards are as high as his grandfather, George VI, who was rated one of the finest shots in the royal household. He and Philip go shooting at Sandringham for pheasant and partridge and in North Yorkshire and Scotland, for grouse. One weekend at Sandringham Charles and Prince Philip, together with a few friends, bagged 600 birds between them.

Father and eldest son also have a love of flying. Philip has clocked up several thousand hours as a pilot all over the world. He has flown almost every type of aircraft, from helicopter to sea-plane and even trans-Atlantic airliners. With his skills in a cockpit he not only encouraged Charles' flying instincts but helped him with advice.

When Prince Philip or Prince Charles go flying, either by helicopter or in fixed-wing aircraft, they travel in the most carefully monitored airspace in Britain. They are given a flight path exclusive to themselves and no other aircraft is allowed to enter or cross it. That section of the sky becomes known as the Purple Airway, out of bounds to even a plane or helicopter on a mercy mission.

Wherever they fly in Britain they often pilot one of the royal helicopters, which, in their red livery, are a common sight over central London. Recently Prince Charles left myself and a few others he had been chatting to in Buckingham Palace to walk to a helicopter parked in the garden, in which he whizzed off in grand style to Wales for the afternoon.

Prince Philip gave up playing competitive polo in 1971, but since then has taken up the fiery pursuit of racing horse-drawn carriages.

One of the greatest pleasures for all the family is putting on old clothes to go for lonely walks over moorlands or through woods. They indulge their love of outdoor life by heading for the hills and moors as often as possible when they stay at Sandringham or Balmoral.

The number of relations now involved in royal duties is a tremendous help to The Queen. They are of different age groups and personalities, covering a wide aspect of interests and, therefore, able to take part in a range of royal involvement she would never hope to achieve alone. Apart from the demands on her time, there are some activities which would be out of character – yet the other recruits can fit in very easily. Prince Charles, for example, is a natural choice for something dangerous or adventurous, while Prince Alexandra and her husband, the Honourable Angus Ogilvy, a successful financier, are perfect for links with the business community.

What might be called a mini-court now exists around the Queen. First in the complicated order of who should represent her on official duties is, of course, Prince Philip, followed by Prince Charles.

Until Prince Edward and Prince Andrew reach the ages when they too can play their full part in the monarchy, Princess Anne and husband, Captain Mark Phillips, are the most important in the royal line.

Princess Anne never felt that she was in second place to Charles as she grew up, because they have always been so close to each other and she was never over-shadowed. It is not in her nature, anyway, to be a shy, blushing violet. She takes after her father, with a forceful personality, a slightly abrasive attitude to life and a determination not to be bossed around. In fact, when they were children it was Anne who was the bossy younger sister to Charles.

It has been difficult for her to fit into the romantic public-relations role of the "Princess Charming". She has never wanted to be a plastic figure satisfying the demands of a Hollywood-style image of a princess. She has made it clear from her teenage days that she is an intelligent human being in her own right who wishes to be accepted for what she is, rather than for what fairy-tale dreamers may wish her to be.

She was born on a sunny August day in 1950 at Clarence House, eighteen months before her mother succeeded to the throne. Anne, the only one of the children not to be born in Buckingham Palace, is fourth in line after her brothers.

The strong steel-fibre of her backbone soon began to show itself when she was barely a toddler. Prince Charles, the sensitive child, would go into a shell after any harsh words of discipline, while Anne virtually ignored attempts at chastisement and continued on her own merry way.

It is not surprising that someone who is such a formidable opponent in horse-riding events today did not bother much with dolls, preferring a tree-climbing, mud-pie, tomboy childhood. She liked playing with and looking after the Queen's famous corgis and soon followed her mother's enthusiasm for horses.

(The Queen has around ten corgis, all of whom are descended from one named Susan, who was so popular with her that she took her on honeymoon. Whenever she is at any of her royal homes, the Queen makes sure she is free around 4.30 each afternoon to feed her dogs, which now include black labradors, with a mixture of meat, dog biscuits and gravy, which she serves with a silver fork and spoon).

Such was Anne's fiercely independent spirit that she disliked staying at home while her brother went away for his education. Eventually Anne was allowed what she had been demanding for so long when, at the age of 13, she was sent to boarding school. After school, and by the time she reached 18, Anne clearly showed she was not only a product of the palace, but also typical of her era – the swinging 60's and early 70's. She seemed to make it clear from the very start in her public life that she valued her independence and felt she should be able to do whatever she wished without succumbing to pressures. She was a typical girl of her time.

She set a style of her own during her late teens and early 20's as far as fashion was concerned, favouring delicate ruffled formal dresses which were not too way-out, or at the other extreme, the ubiquitous sweaters and jeans. Once again, showing her determination to be seen and appreciated as herself, rather than the result of image-making, she did not try to become what was unnatural to her – be a "swinger" or trend-setter. She was at her happiest in private with her family, especially indulging in their country-life activities. Riding became, and still is, the activity that overshadows all her other interests.

From childhood she was always a courageous and natural horsewoman and the older she got the better became the quality of animal that her mother and father provided her with. "Anne only seemed to live when she was on one of her ponies or later on a full-size horse," a former member of the court said recently. To her, riding was a perfect way in which she could establish herself in international competition as someone to be reckoned with for her own skills– not because she was a member of the Royal Family.

During her early days among horses she was reluctant to learn the finer points of riding expertise. The monotonous repetition of training bored her, as did the nuisance of having to look after the animals. Because she wished to excel in the field, however, she eventually agreed to learn the skills of horsemanship – efforts which have since paid off with the number of national and international awards she has gained.

After the usual girlish round of local gymkhanas the princess entered what could be called the Big League of the horse world in 1971, the tough Badminton three-day horse trials. This is a complicated test presenting horses and riders with every possible demand from dressage, to a tough cross-country obstacle course and show jumping. Anne came through this and other tests magnificently and as a result was chosen to represent Britain in international events, including the 1976 Olympic Games in Montreal. She tackled the 36 fence cross-country course with her usual courage but halfway round she fell. Although shaken and lying on the ground for several minutes she re-mounted and finished the course, but it was of little use. She had too many faults to help the British team, which, in any case, had a bad running all round in that year's Games.

Away from the show-ring the Princess involves herself in charity work. She works very hard, as president, of the Save The Children Fund and is the patron for a charity close to her heart, the Riding for the Disabled Association, to which she devotes a lot of her time.

Anne, unlike her brother, had never been the subject of much gossip or speculation on romance. She had few boyfriends and it was through her love of horses that she met someone who could share her life.

She first met Captain Mark Phillips when she went with the Queen Mother to a reception in the late summer of 1968 for Britain's team in that year's Olympic Games. She had just left school and was not on anyone's marital list, but over the years they saw more of each other on the horse-show circuit. Mark, a dashing young Army subaltern, was a member of the British equestrian team which won gold medals at the Munich Olympics in 1972, which Anne attended as a spectator.

They soon began to spend a lot of time together outside the show-ring and after a year of secret courtship they announced their engagement in May 1973. The son of a country-squire businessman and the daughter of a Queen married on a chilly November morning that year. Anne became for the first time the fairy-tale princess as, in her wedding dress, she drove with her father in a glass coach through streets lined with thousands of well-wishers to Westminster Abbey. The coach had been used by her mother and father on their wedding day and her long veil was held in place by a tiara that the Queen had also worn for her wedding. Before the wedding Mark said: "I just love everything about her".

Mark, who is two years older than Anne, comes from a long line of military men and a family who live very much in the country style in a sixteenth century manor house in Wiltshire. After their marriage Anne became a soldier's wife, living with Mark in quarters at Sandhurst Military Academy, where he was an instructor, but their original interest in riding did not die. They became a regular and popular couple at riding events throughout Britain and abroad.

Four years almost to the day after their wedding, Princess Anne gave birth to her first child, Peter. She set a number of breaks from royal tradition. She decided to go into a public hospital, St. Mary's in Paddington, in one of the grimmer suburbs in London, and young Peter became the first baby so near to the throne to be born in hospital. After his birth, both Anne and Mark insisted that Peter, named after his paternal grandfather, should not be given a title – another royal first.

Since the arrival of their child Anne and Mark have begun to set up a home of their own in magnificent Gatcombe Park in Gloucestershire, a stone-built mansion built in the eighteenth century which stands in 750 acres. It was bought for them at a price of three-quarters of a million pounds by the Queen. It is a considerable change from their first home after marriage, which was rented Army accommodation costing £8 per week.

Now that they have begun to lay the foundations for a new branch of the family, Anne and Mark look to a future as farming folk and estate owners.

Mark has left the Army, with regret, because his marriage was a drawback to any promotion he could expect to the top ranks of his career. Any officer in the British Army today has got to have experience in Northern Ireland, among combat conditions. Because the husband of the fourth in line to the throne, and father of the fifth in succession, was such a prime target for a specific terrorist attack or kidnapping, he would never have been allowed to go there. The only alternative for Mark, who did not wish to stay for ever at the bottom of the military tree, was to resign his commission.

There are many dangers that the royal security men cannot ignore, especially as far as Mark and Anne are concerned.

They were the targets for a violent kidnap attempt one spring evening in 1974 when they were driving along the Mall to the palace after being guests of honour at a film show. A 26-year old man, Ian Ball, subsequently found to be mentally unstable, swung his small family car in front of the royal limousine, forcing it to stop, and came out waving two guns. He came face to face first of all with the incredibly brave royal bodyguard, Scotland Yard Inspector James Beaton, whom Ball shot in the chest. The policeman drew his gun, which jammed after one shot but, though wounded, he still tried to tackle the attacker and did not give up the fight until he collapsed on the ground having been wounded twice more. How he ever survived his wounds is remarkable.

Next to be shot was the royal chauffeur, Alexander Callender, who was wounded in the chest as he tried to grab the gun. A third victim was a Fleet Street journalist, Mr Brian McConnell, who jumped from a passing taxi and tried to persuade Ball to hand over the gun. McConnell was severely wounded by a shot in the chest. By now more people, including police, had reached the scene and Ball fled into nearby St. James' Park, where he was brought down by an unarmed constable. Police later found adequate evidence that Ball intended to kidnap the princess and demand a £3 million ransom. He was sent to a security hospital "without limit of time".

Mark and Anne are now concentrating on building up and administering the Gatcombe Park estate, where, apart from breeding high quality cattle, they intend to train horses for show jumping and competition. The house has a fine row of recently renovated stables.

An indoor training ring will be used for year-round work with the horses, and the estate is nicely placed for riding and hunting. It is in the area of one of the finest hunts in England, the Beaufort, and not far away from the venue of the Badminton Horse Trials. Anne is competing as hard as ever since the birth of Peter and she is still a keen huntswoman.

One of the hardest working members of the "outer court" is the Duke of Gloucester, a cousin of the Queen who is ninth in the order of succession. A family tragedy brought him closer to royal duties. As Prince Richard, the second son of Elizabeth's late uncle, he never expected to inherit land, riches or the responsibilities of links with the monarchy. By nature he is a quiet, affable man, slightly shy, and one who always wanted a secluded life away from pomp and ceremony. He had trained at Cambridge as an architect, and always intended to make his own, unobtrusive, way in the world. He met his wife, Birgitte van Deurs, the daughter of a Danish lawyer, at a tea party while he was at university. She was studying English at a Cambridge language school. Both of them tended to be modest in their ways, so they never wanted a big fuss made of their wedding three years later in 1972. Instead of a traditional royal affair in Westminster Abbey, the marriage ceremony, and church chosen, matched the simple sort of life they both prefer. It was a village wedding in the thirteenth century church at Barnwell in Northamptonshire, the ancestral home of the Gloucesters. Such was the restrained simplicity of the occasion that Richard's mother, the Duchess, arranged the flowers in the church.

He and blonde Birgitte seemed all set for an unsophisticated life as a working couple – he as an architect and she in business – when the elder brother, Prince William, was killed in a plane crash. The tragedy happened only two months after their wedding. William, a dashing sort of fellow with a fondness for fast cars, aircraft and a hectic existence,

was destined to inherit the estate and the position so close to the throne. He had trained as a diplomat with the Foreign Office and was well used to public life, but a light aircraft he was piloting suddenly swooped to the ground soon after take off and burst into flames.

Two years later, in 1974, the old duke died and Richard and his new wife were thrust into a public role they never sought. In spite of this they now play their full part in carrying out royal duties.

Another wife who was never trained for the task, but who has taken to it with great aplomb, is the Duchess of Kent, the graceful companion of another of the Queen's cousins. She was born Katharine Worsley, daughter of Sir William Worsley, a family of Yorkshire county stock. Katharine had met the duke when he was serving with his cavalry regiment, the Royal Scots Greys, not far away from her home, Hovingham Hall in North Yorkshire.

She was at first reluctant to commit herself to marriage with the young duke, because it would mean becoming so closely linked with the throne. Eventually she accepted that the restrictions of stately life would have to be put up with, and they married in York Minster in 1961. Since then she has taken on more than her fair share of the royal workload and, for someone not born in a palace, has taken to the life with all the charm and expertise of a princess.

A princess who was born to the job, but married in reverse, so to speak, is Princess Alexandra, the vivacious daughter of the late Duke of Kent and Princess Marina of Greece. "Alex" met a man who was far from the royal crowd, the Honourable Angus Ogilvy, son of the twelfth Earl of Airlie, but essentially a young thrusting businessman making his way in the City of London. Because he is heavily committed to his career in finance, the couple have a very efficient working relationship as far as official duties are concerned. Princess Alexandra meets a busy working diary generally alone, except when it would be normally expected that a husband and wife would be together – at dinners, premieres, weddings and church services, for example.

The princess always seems to be so happy with life and has a ready smile whenever she appears in public – qualities that have made her one of the best liked of the Queen's relatives.

Not quite waiting on the wings – more likely popping his head round the curtains – and impatient to get fully involved in public life, is Prince Andrew, the Queen's second son.

If Charles tends to take after his mother in his personality, Andrew is truly a chip off the old block. He is a strapping six-footer, having all the exuberance of youth, as well as the fearless, sand-paperish characteristics of his father. With his striking good looks, he is also, much to his delight, being dubbed by the media as the new royal "pin-up boy".

He is more extrovert than Charles, yet has the Queen Mother's crowd-pleasing charm. He is very open and frank, and fond of using sometimes excruciatingly corny jokes to break the ice with people he meets.

From early on he was a boisterous child; even as a toddler he would drive the palace staff mad with his mischievous ways and determination to get his own way every time.

As soon as he was out of the nursery Prince Philip

set him on the same path as brother Charles twelve years earlier: gymnastics, riding and swimming – activities which Andrew took to with more enthusiasm than Charles did at the age of five. He only needed about half-an-hour to get the hang of swimming and was soon racing down the palace pool with his father.

By the time Andrew went to Gordonstoun at the age of thirteen the staff were claiming that it was less Spartan than in Charles' day. Showers were no longer compulsory in winter, and girls had been admitted as an experiment in co-educaton. A great value was still placed on the hardiness of life, however, and Andrew accepted the whole thing with zest. He wrote glowing letters home after only a few months there.

With an aggressiveness inherited from his father it was to be expected that he would land himself in the odd quarrel, and masters recall that he was good with his fists. He became what Gordonstoun likes to turn out, a good all rounder in the British public school tradition – someone who was good academically yet could still wield a straight bat on the sports field. He fitted in easily with the tough regime of Gordonstoun.

He has enormous physical energy and courage, and is now developing into a greater daredevil than his elder brother.

By the age of eighteen he had already proven himself to be a tough opponent on the rugby field, a first-rate yachtsman, an excellent skier, an almost reckless ice-hockey player and a qualified glider pilot.

Flight Lieutenant Peter Bullivant, the man who trained Andrew to glide while at Gordonstoun recalls: "He learnt fast, really fast. I am not saying that because he is a prince. It really is so. The only thing that stopped him from getting his licence as a glider pilot in a record time up here in Scotland was due to the fact that we had to wait for his 16th birthday. He was ready for it within weeks, and to celebrate his birthday he went solo for the first time."

The Queen and her advisers have always thought it essential for the royal sons to spend some period of their education in the Commonwealth.

Charles went to Timbertops in Australia and the experience was not only successful in cementing Commonwealth relations but it also brought out all the best that we now see in Charles. He often says: "I grew up in Australia". It has become one of his favourite countries, which he always enjoys visiting and he regards it as a second home.

Canada was to be the place for Andrew. Lakefield College, about 100 miles east of Toronto and a school which had an exchange scheme with Gordonstoun, was chosen for the prince.

The six months spent there by Andrew, with his love of the outdoors and hardy physical activities, became more like a holiday than an educational chore. He improved his skiing on the snow-covered hills around the school, and went on an adventure trek and canoeing expedition in the wild north of Canada.

He could not resist making clear his reputation as a comedian soon after reaching Lakefield. He told 16-year-old Peter Dance, the boy taking his place at Gordonstoun: "It's like a prison out there. Like being cooped up in a war-time camp like Colditz. The mattresses are a thin layer of old straw. The beds are hard as iron. The food is terrible". It was a perturbed Peter who headed across the Atlantic, where, fortuitously, his worst fears were not realised.

Andrew had been taught to ice skate when he was seven years old but ice-hockey at Lakefield was a new experience. At first he had to take some mighty spills, leaving him with a mass of bruises.

When he arrived at Lakefield there was a reaction among some of the boys there who declared that they would "push in the royal nose". On the ice-rink Andrew came up against experienced schoolboy players in this roughest and sometimes dirtiest of all sports. He seized the initiative right from the beginning and laid about them with such verve that the referee warned him about "rough play". One of the survivors of the onslaught said admiringly later: "He is no English gentleman – he plays dirty".

Andrew made the most of his half year in North America. He did not just stay in Canada. On one occasion he travelled with a party of his schoolmates 600 miles in a chartered bus to Pittsburgh to watch the Pittsburgh Penguins play ice-hockey. He was fascinated by what he saw on the journey, constantly asking questions about the American way of life. At Pittsburgh he spent two nights in a local hotel – heavily guarded all the time by his personal detective, and a Mountie sent from Canada.

The Queen wishes to keep Andrew out of the public eye until he finishes his education, but he is gradually being brought to the fore. His first big formal occasion was at the Montreal Olympics when he was among the royal party at the games.

He is mad about sport, and at Montreal he, alone among the Royals, wanted to see every sport he could. When his parents returned to their quarters Andrew insisted on staying around to watch whatever sport was still going on.

One of Andrew's greatest ventures so far is becoming a fully-trained parachutist. I noticed his cool courage when he took the ten-day "para" course with the Royal Air Force in the spring of 1978. He was not given any special privileges because he was a prince – he had to go through all the arduous training and take the same risks as the other members of the crack Parachute Regiment who were with him.

During one of his early jumps from a Hercules aircraft at a thousand feet over South Cerney in Gloucestershire, the slipstream of the plane flung him into a spin, twisting his parachute rigging into a tangle. He jerked and bounced his body on the end of the 'chute until it was free, made a text-book landing and said calmly: "That was great – I can't wait to get up again". Was he scared? "Yes, of course – if you're not scared and nervous you'll do something stupid," he answered.

What will happen next to Andrew? He may go to university but a career in the Royal Air Force or Royal Navy seems certain. He may experience them both, as Charles has done. Whatever he does, neither Andrew nor his lifestyle will be boring.

This then is what the world regards as its first family – even citizens of countries with their own monarchies still look to the British Royal Family with admiration and affection.

They cover four generations which are a living link going back to the Victorian Age – eighty years of glorious pageantry behind them and every indication of a greater future ahead.

As the man said: "They're such a nice family to be with."

An early photograph *above* taken in 1926, of the baby Princess Elizabeth seated on the lap of her mother, the then Duchess of York – who was destined to become Queen Elizabeth and then the Queen Mother. (Marcus Adams)

The group *above right* comprises King George V and Queen Mary with the Dukes of York, Gloucester and Kent and the Prince of Wales. (Bassano)

The photograph *right* was taken on the 27th July 1927 and shows, from the left: King George V and Queen Mary (seated): the Duke of York (who succeeded his brother Edward VIII as King George VI in 1937) and the Duchess of York (later Queen Elizabeth) with the fourteen-month-old Princess Elizabeth on her knee. Extreme right, standing, are the 14th Earl of Strathmore and the Countess of Strathmore, parents of the Duchess of York. (Bassano)

Overleaf. A formal study *left* typical of the time, 1931, of the five year-old Princess Elizabeth and *right* Princess Elizabeth, aged two, held by her mother, the then Duchess of York, in 1928. (Marcus Adams)

In 1927, at the age of one year, the then Princess Elizabeth posed *above* with her Grandmother, Her Majesty Queen Mary, for her first birthday portrait. (Marcus Adams)

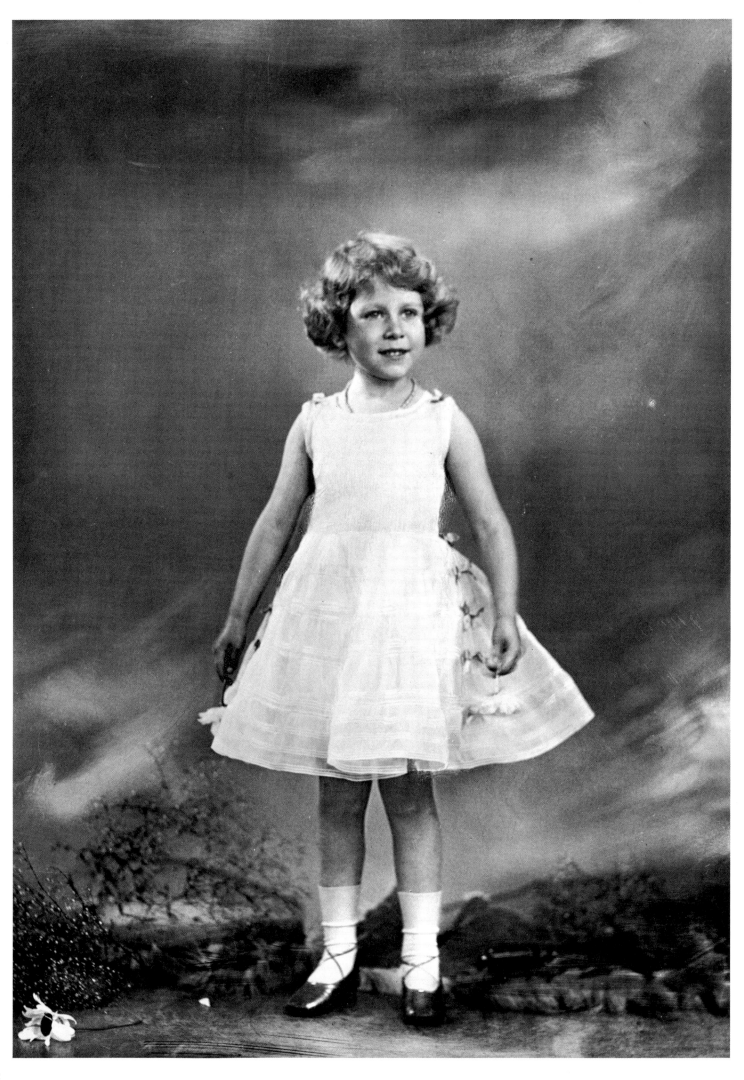

Top. A Royal trio photographed in 1934: HRH the Duchess of York with her two daughters when Princess Elizabeth *left* was eight years old and her sister, Princess Margaret *right* was four. (Marcus Adams)

In June 1936 the two Royal Princesses were photographed *above* playing with the family's pet corgis in the grounds of the Royal Lodge, Windsor. HRH Princess Elizabeth was ten and HRH Princess Margaret was nearly six. Their uncle King Edward VIII had yet to be crowned but by the end of that year would have abdicated in favour of their father, who became King George VI. (Studio Lisa)

The Royal Lodge, Windsor was the setting, in 1942, for the picture *right* of His Majesty King George VI with his two daughters – Princess Margaret, then aged eleven, on the left and fifteen year-old Princess Elizabeth on the right. (Studio Lisa)

The charming family group *above*, taken in 1939, shows King George VI, Queen Elizabeth and their daughters Princess Elizabeth *left* and the young Princess Margaret *right*. The family had lived quietly on the fringes of royal activity until 1936, when they moved to the centre of the stage on the succession of King George VI, and Princess Elizabeth learned that one day she might well be Queen. (Marcus Adams)

Two formal wartime portraits *left* and *above left* of the royal sisters taken in 1941. Quite unlike the more natural photographs we see today, they nevertheless have a charm and dignity that is very much of their time. (Marcus Adams)

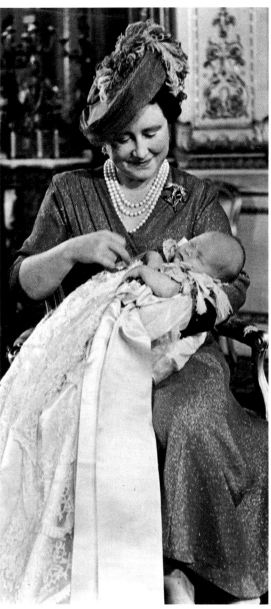

In 1942, shortly after becoming Colonel of the Grenadier Guards, Princess Elizabeth posed for the portrait *above*. (Cecil Beaton)

The news of the birth of a son to the then Princess Elizabeth on the fourteenth of November 1948 created an understandable request for photographs and he was duly pictured with his mother *above left*, in Buckingham Palace; with both his parents *far right top*, and with an obviously delighted grandmother, Queen Elizabeth *above*. (Cecil Beaton)

As the years passed, so the pictures took on a more relaxed look. The picture *near right, top* shows Princess Elizabeth with her second child, Princess Anne, who was born only one month previously, on August 15th 1950. A slightly apprehensive two year old Prince Charles is shown with his mother *far right bottom*. An obvious interest in things mechanical is displayed by Her Majesty's two younger sons, Prince Edward and Prince Andrew, photographed *near right, centre* with their mother, Queen Elizabeth II, at Windsor Castle in 1965. (Cecil Beaton, Studio Lisa)

The formal study *left* was taken to commemorate the christening of Prince Charles. Seated on the then Princess Elizabeth's left is her grandmother, Queen Mary. (Baron)

31

A charming mixture of the formal and the informal.
The three regal studies *right* provide an effective contrast
to the informality of the photographs of Prince Philip,
Princess Elizabeth and their children Prince Charles and
Princess Anne *top*, Queen Elizabeth–now the Queen
Mother–with her daughters Princess Margaret and
Princess Elizabeth *centre* and the Queen, Prince Philip,
Prince Charles, Princess Anne and the baby Prince
Andrew in the grounds of Balmoral *above* in 1960.
(Studio Lisa, Dorothy Wilding, Karsh)

The portrait of Her Majesty *far left* was taken during Coronation Year, 1953 and that on the *left* was taken in the Green Drawing Room at Buckingham Palace and was a Royal Command Portrait, as was the photograph *far left, below* which shows the Queen on the small staircase in the Grand Entrance of Buckingham Palace. (Dorothy Wilding, Baron)

The picture of the Queen *below* is very reminiscent of the famous painting by Annigoni, and Her Majesty is shown *right* in her Coronation robes, on Coronation Day, June 2nd, 1953. (Cecil Beaton)

The elegantly sombre portrait *below centre* of Her Majesty Queen Elizabeth–now the Queen Mother–was taken in 1948. (Cecil Beaton)

All the pictures on these pages were taken during the 1950's. In the portrait *above* of the Queen and the Duke of Edinburgh, taken in the Grand Entrance in Buckingham Palace, Her Majesty is wearing the Ribbon and Star of the Garter and the Duke is seen in the uniform of Admiral of the Fleet. (Baron)

The young Queen with her young family *right* photographed when she was twenty-six, only a year after she had succeeded to the throne on the death of her father.
(Marcus Adams)

The picture of the Queen and Prince Philip *far left* was taken on the circular landing above the Grand Staircase in Buckingham Palace. (Donald McKague)

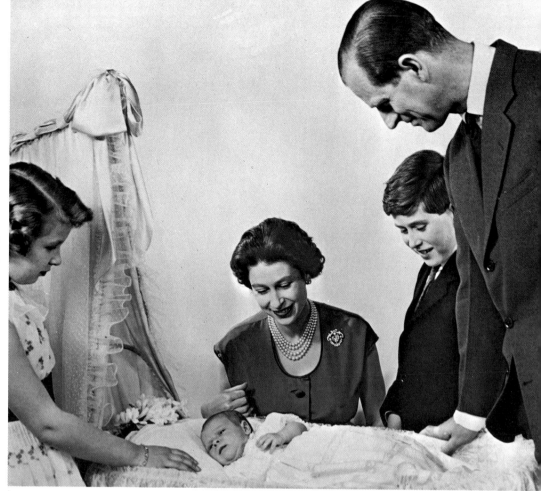

The delight that a new addition to the family brings is clear from the charming pictures on these pages which show Her Majesty's fourth child, Prince Edward, *left* who was born on March 10th 1964; the crib is the same one that was used for the Queen and Princess Margaret and has since been used for all the Queen's children.

The new baby in the pictures *right* is the Royal Family's second son Prince Andrew, who arrived on the 19th February, 1960. (Cecil Beaton)

The Duchess of York, who was later to become Queen Elizabeth and eventually the Queen Mother, has always been a favourite member of the Royal Family with people from all walks of life all over the world.

The Queen Mother is portrayed *left* in the Drawing Room of Clarence House wearing the sash of the Order of the Garter and the Garter Star, together with the Family Orders. (Cecil Beaton)

Both the pictures *above* were taken to celebrate the Queen Mother's seventieth birthday on the 4th August 1970. (Cecil Beaton)

Another birthday, five years later, was the occasion when the photograph *right* was taken of the Queen Mother with her grandson Prince Charles. (Peter Sellars)

As the years pass we begin to see more and more natural photographs. Even though some of them are, strictly speaking, posed, they still have a feeling of informality about them and they show us the Royal Family with the emphasis on the family rather than the royal.

The photograph *left* shows the Queen in the gardens of her London home, Buckingham Palace. (Dmitri Kasterine)

Prince Philip provides the Queen with a graphic, and apparently amusing, description *below* of his performance in the four-in-hand driving Grand Prix at Windsor.

Two happy and relaxed family groups show *right* the Royal Family at Balmoral in 1972 and *below right* the Queen and Prince Philip with their two younger sons, Prince Andrew (right) and Prince Edward (centre). (Lichfield, Godfrey Argent)

Four-in-hand Carriage driving is a sport that Prince Philip has taken up in recent years, and at which he now excels. The sport is a demanding one requiring co-operation between team and driver, great skill and long hours of practice. The Royal Windsor Horse Show provides Prince Philip with a chance to exercise his skills in dressage *left* and cross-country *right*, and obviously provides enjoyment for the Queen *above*.
(Serge Lemoine)

The beautiful picture *left* which looks as though it had been taken in a quiet, rural area is, in fact, in the heart of London, in the grounds of Buckingham Palace. It portrays the Queen and Prince Philip with their children Prince Charles and Princess Anne in 1957. (Snowdon)

Windsor Castle during Jubilee Year, 1977, was the setting for the delightful photographs *above, above right* and *right* of Her Majesty the Queen and Prince Philip. (Chris Smith)

The Queen and Master Peter Phillips, her first grandson,
photographed at Windsor Castle on the 5th April 1978. (Snowdon)

The early years

The young Queen Elizabeth the Second, pictured at Windsor in 1954. (Studio Lisa)

Overleaf. Two studies by Karsh of Ottawa. The photograph *right* was taken in 1943, when Princess Elizabeth was seventeen.

Coming so soon after the gloom of the Second World War, the marriage of Princess Elizabeth, King George VI's elder daughter, to Lieutenant Philip Mountbatten, provided a much-needed touch of glamour and happiness.

The wedding took place in Westminster Abbey on the 20th November, 1947 and the bride wore an ivory satin dress designed by Norman Hartnell. The full skirt was embroidered with flowers picked out in seed pearls and crystal. The white tulle head-dress was held in place by a pearl and diamond tiara and the Princess carried a bouquet of white orchids. (Baron)

His Royal Highness Prince Charles was born on the 14th November, 1948 and the first photograph of the family together *below* was taken in Buckingham Palace when the baby was nineteen weeks old. (Baron)

Four Royal generations are featured in the photograph *bottom left* which was taken in the Music Room at Buckingham Palace following the christening ceremony of Prince Charles. King George VI is shown standing behind his mother, Queen Mary and his daughter the then Princess Elizabeth with the baby Prince Charles on her knee. (Baron)

The photograph *left* was taken in 1950 and shows the Royal couple with their two children, Prince Charles and Princess Anne. (Baron)

The pictures on this page show: *left* The young Princess Anne in Brownie uniform, *right* Prince Andrew and Prince Edward in the Music Room at Buckingham Palace, *below* the Queen and Princess Anne at Windsor, in 1959, *bottom right* the Queen with her youngest son, Prince Edward. One of the first occasions on which the Queen's youngest child, Prince Edward, was seen was when he left London with his mother and brother, Prince Andrew, en route for Windsor *bottom*. The picture *centre left* shows the Queen with Prince Edward in the Royal train.

Her Majesty the Queen with
Princess Anne and one of the
family corgis at Windsor in
1959 *left* (Studio Lisa)

The picture *below* shows the
Queen, very much in the role of
a mother, with her young son
Prince Andrew. (Studio Lisa)

A few years separate the three
pictures on the right. The
garden setting *right* and the
rather more formal indoor
study *centre right* both show
Her Majesty and Prince Philip
with their children Prince
Charles, Princess Anne, Prince
Andrew and Prince Edward.
The photograph *bottom right*
features the Queen and Prince
Philip with their two younger
sons, Prince Andrew and
Prince Edward.
(Keith McMillan)

Her Majesty the Queen, photographed in 1960 *above* by Cecil Beaton, who also took the splendid picture *right* of Her Majesty with Prince Philip.

The tradition of a great occasion *above* as Her Majesty presides over the opening of a new session of Parliament in 1958. (Cecil Beaton)

Ceremony and Pageantry

Unique traditions and glorious pageantry keep the monarchy alive with a ceremonial splendour seen nowhere else in the world.

Whether it be the pomp of the State Opening of Parliament or the simple giving of the specially minted silver Maundy Money coins to old people every year, the Queen carries everything off with a style that has millions gasping with admiration.

The Royal Family enjoys dressing up for a great occasion: the chance to drive through banner-hung streets, and taking part in ceremonies that are living proof of the continuity of rule.

One of the highspots of the royal year for the Queen is Trooping the Colour or the Queen's Birthday Parade. Being a monarch she is allowed to have two birthdays each year – her natural anniversary (April 21) and an official one, which usually falls on the first Saturday in June.

This is the day when 1,600 officers and men in her five regiments of footguards and two regiments of horseguards, march and trot on Horse Guards Parade, off Whitehall, in intricate patterns that take six weeks to rehearse. There is a twisting movement of the mass bands that is so complicated that it can never be written down on paper – the skill is handed down by word of mouth through generations of drill sergeants.

Parading regimental colours goes back more than 200 years to when the flag would be carried among the soldiers on the eve of a battle so that they could recognise it as a rallying point among the smoke, fire and slaughter.

Ceremonially parading the colours of a guards battalion – embroidered with battle honours – before the sovereign began in 1805 and it has continued annually ever since. The Queen has made a point, throughout her reign, of leading her troops off the parade ground and along The Mall. She rides side-saddle on a police horse that has been trained to behave placidly amid all the din of the military bands and the cheering and shouting.

One of the greatest constitutional functions Her Majesty performs each year is the State Opening of Parliament. This is the occasion when it is formally accepted that it is "Her Majesty's Government". After a procession through the streets from Buckingham Palace to Westminster she sits before the robed Peers in the House of Lords and reads a statement of what HER government intends to do in the way of legislation in the coming year. It is a ceremony going back to the days of William the Conqueror, who told the bishops, earls and barons of his day what he expected them to do. Although the Queen's Speech is couched in such terms that it appears she is instructing the Government what to do, it is, in fact, a policy statement prepared by the Prime Minister. Members of the House of Commons are also allowed – on this one day – to stand at the door of the Upper House to hear the speech.

It is the Queen, of course, who confers the great honours of Peerage and Knighthood at ceremonies held mainly at Buckingham Palace, but she often dubs a knight with her sword during tours abroad. She has also been known to perform the act of knighthood with a close friend privately at one of the royal homes, and in 1967 she tapped round-the-world yachtsman Sir Francis Chichester on the shoulders alongside the Thames at Greenwich. Formal investitures are held fourteen times a year in the State Ballroom at Buckingham Palace. The velvet covered stool used for the recipient to kneel on has been used for this purpose for sixty years.

The greatest honour the Queen can bestow is her personal Order of the Garter. There are only 24 Knight Companions at any one time, who have the privilege of wearing the garter insignia on their left breast with the inscription "Honi soit qui mal y pense" (Shame on him who thinks evil of it). King Edward III used these words after he picked up the blue garter of Joan, Countess of Salisbury, when she lost it while he was dancing with her in April 1348. He said this to silence snickering courtiers…and from this has come the oldest order of chivalry in Britain.

Taking part in much of the royal pageantry are some of the more colourful of the Queen's escorts, the Yeomen of the Guard. They wear bright red costumes that have not changed since the days of Henry the Eighth, who founded the corps. It is the oldest military regiment in the world. To join this exclusive band of bodyguards a man has to have served at least 22 years in one of the services, reached a non-commissioned or warrant officer rank, have a good conduct medal and must have fought in at least one campaign. Although they no longer carry out these functions, but hold the titles as a mark of honour, four of them are "Yeoman Bed Hangers" while another four are "Yeoman Bed Goers". The jobs were created by King Henry, who trusted nobody. Their original duties were to check the curtains hanging round the royal bed for any possible assassins and to turn the straw mattress to search for hidden knives or swords.

They now have the no less important duty of walking alongside the Queen on ceremonial occasions, carrying pike-staffs.

Dating from 1349, "The Most Noble and Amiable Company of St. George named the Garter" is the oldest order of Christian chivalry in Britain. Originally the order comprised only twenty-five Knights, but this number was increased in 1831 to allow the Prince of Wales and other members of the British and foreign Royal Families to be admitted.

The Garter Ceremony, at which new Knights are invested, takes place at Windsor Castle, following which the Knights of the Order walk to St. George's Chapel, preceded by the Military Knights of Windsor and various heralds. A service is then held in the chapel, after which the Queen and her family return in open carriages to the castle.

The ceremony is very colourful and it takes place in a very beautiful and historic location. There is little wonder, therefore, that large crowds of sightseers are always attracted to it.

Overleaf. The Queen and Prince Philip leading the Garter Ceremony procession.

Trooping the Colour – Her Majesty's official birthday – is always held on a Saturday in June. It is both a highlight of the British tourist season and a regular fixture in the Queen's year.

Certainly the most spectacular of the large number of events the Queen attends, Trooping the Colour always draws huge crowds. This was particularly so in Silver Jubilee Year. In the picture *below*, the Queen and her family are shown on the balcony of Buckingham Palace, watching the fly-past of the Royal Air Force.
(Serge Lemoine)

Overleaf. Some of the scenes that make the Trooping the Colour Ceremony the fascinating spectacle that it is.

Pageantry obviously plays a large and important part in the Royal Family's calendar. There have always been those who argue that such pageantry is an unnecessary expense and should be abolished – and yet more visitors come to Britain because of its pageantry and traditions than for any other reason. At such spectacles as Trooping the Colour, Changing the Guard and all the many other ceremonies involving troops, mounted or on foot, Beefeaters and even Chelsea Pensioners, there are always large crowds of onlookers, many of them from overseas. (Serge Lemoine)

Even when there is no event taking place, people still gather outside Buckingham Palace simply, perhaps, to look at the Queen's London home.

Her Majesty, pictured *overleaf* with her Yeoman Warders at the Tower of London.

pages 74, 75, 76 and 77. More scenes from the Trooping the Colour and the Order of the Garter Ceremonies.

Her Majesty wearing the Mantle of The Most Ancient and Noble Order of
The Thistle.
By Leonard Boden, R.P., F.R.S.A.

Royal portraits

Douglas Anderson's 1964 portrait of the Queen caused considerable
controversy when it first appeared.

Simon Elwes' magnificent painting of the Queen was commissioned by the President and Officers of the Wardroom Mess, the Royal Naval Barracks, Portsmouth.

This portrait of Her Majesty was painted for the Royal Air Force by Henry Carr; it hangs in the
Air Council Chamber of the Air Ministry building in Whitehall.

Pietro Annigoni's first portrait of the Queen *far left* was painted in 1954. His second portrait *right* shows the Queen at 43 and is in striking contrast to the romanticism of the earlier work.

The painting *left* is by Sir William Hutchison for the Auckland Savings Bank, New Zealand, and *below* is seen the mature and regal portrait by Anthony Devas, A.R.A., R.P. *Bottom left* is the work by Denis Fildes; a life-size painting that was presented to the Cutler's Company of Hallamshire by Thomas Ward Ltd, of Sheffield.

The outstanding photographs on these pages and overleaf were all taken by that master of portrait photography, Karsh of Ottawa, in the White Drawing Room at Buckingham Palace.

The photographs *above and left* were taken by Peter Grugeon, as was the picture *overleaf right* of His Royal Highness the Duke of Edinburgh.

The Study *overleaf left* is by Karsh of Ottawa and shows Prince Charles at the age of 27. The photograph was taken at the residence of the Governor General of Canada in Ottawa.

Pages 92 and 93. Left An informal portrait of Prince Edward taken by John Scott and *right* Prince Andrew at eighteen years, by Peter Grugeon.

The Queen Mother

The Queen Mother has the warmest and most famous smile in the world, with enough cheerfulness in her manner to make her everyone's favourite grandmother.

Queen Elizabeth the appropriately-titled Queen Mother, is now seventy eight years old but shows no signs of putting on a royal shawl and retiring from public life. She is as busy as she ever was and still holds a special place in the affections of millions.

She is a remarkable woman, who has probably the unique record of having been the daughter-in-law of one king, the sister-in-law of another, the wife of another, the mother of a queen and is now happily seeing the maturing of a grandson who will be a future king.

At an age when some women are sitting in armchairs doing their knitting, the Queen Mother is remarkably active, walking over the heather-covered moors of her beloved Scotland, standing up to her waist in fast-flowing water casting for salmon, or carrying out a hectic round of official duties. "I love meeting people," she frequently tells those who ask how she manages to keep up such a dashing pace. "Most people are really very nice, you know."

She became a queen by an odd quirk of history – the abdication of the Duke of Windsor as Edward VIII. If one believes in fortune tellers, however, she knew her fate from the age of seven, when a gipsy woman held her palm and told her that she would be a queen one day.

Strengthened by a happy marriage to King George VI, she became the perfect consort to a monarch and a mother who created a blissful home life for her husband and children. The happiness among her own family when she was a young princess was taken as an example and encouragement by the Queen when she became both a monarch and mother at Buckingham Palace.

Her six grandchildren and one great-grandchild are now her greatest interest. She has been close to the Queen's four children and Princess Margaret's son and daughter through every step of their lives, and today she has, as well, the joy of Princess Anne's baby. Like grandmas everywhere she did her share of baby-sitting, looking after the youngsters while their parents were on tours abroad, or just making sure they behaved themselves in public.

Prince Charles is her favourite grandson. They have always had a relationship that seems more intimate than the others. During his schooldays Charles kept constantly in touch by phone or letter with his grandmother, who was always ready with a few words of advice and comfort. When he was at school in Australia, and feeling a little homesick, the Queen Mother joined Charles to cheer him up and they went fishing together for a few days in the Snowy Mountains.

Whenever Charles wants to escape from the formalities of his own hectic life he often joins her at one of her two homes in Scotland. Springtime usually finds her at Birkhall, the house and estate in Aberdeenshire, near to Balmoral. It lies near to the River Dee and the Queen Mother believes that that is the time when the water is at its best for fishing.

Throughout her life she has set an elegant style in her dress, especially with her celebrated pearls and hats, yet some of her favourite moments are when she can just wear casual old clothes. Birkhall, Sandringham and Royal Lodge, Windsor, are places where she can get away from the formality of other royal homes and go walking or fishing in baggy, comfortable clothes and rubber boots.

While her eldest daughter is deeply involved in flat racing, the Queen Mother is interested in the more dramatic steeplechasing. She bought her first horse in 1949 and since then has put into training a string of successful jumpers which, over the years, have brought her more than 300 wins. In only her second season she had a great success with a powerful brown horse, Manicou, which won the race named after her husband, the King George the VI Stakes, at Kempton Park. Manicou was put to stud and has sired a generation of successful jumpers.

During the early days the Queen, then Princess Elizabeth, and her mother jointly owned a chaser. The daughter gave up her interest in jumpers, though, after their horse broke a leg and had to be destroyed. The Queen is remembered as being heartbroken and she has never been fond of steeplechasing since.

With her busy official life continuing without any signs of retirement, and her active social activities, the Royal Family is justifiably proud of the lady affectionately known as "the Queen Mum". An American Army sergeant once referred to her as "a swell gal". One of her entourage put it another way when he said recently: "No one comes any better."

Left. Her Majesty Queen Elizabeth the Queen Mother.

The pomp and glitter of first nights, charity premieres, receptions and all the many other functions that are a necessary part of any royal programme are shared by the Queen Mother *right* and her daughters. (Jack Esten)

Princess Margaret is pictured *left* in animated conversation with Liberace.

During her tour of the United States of America the Queen met heavyweight boxing champion Mohammed Ali *bottom left* and, with President Ford, exchanged a few words with Elizabeth Taylor *below*. (Colin Davey).

Overleaf. The Queen Mother shares an amusing moment with Danny La Rue and Ken Dodd.

Pages 100 and 101. Both these pictures were taken in the grounds of Royal Lodge, Windsor, to celebrate the Queen Mother's seventieth birthday on 4th August 1970.

On August 4th 1975 Her Majesty the Queen Mother celebrated her seventy-fifth birthday. For the occasion she was photographed in the drawing room of her London residence, Clarence House. Her Majesty is wearing a full length dress of white chiffon embroidered with patterns of gold beads, a diamond tiara, diamond drop earrings, a diamond bracelet and a pearl and diamond necklace. She is also wearing the Garter Sash and Star with the Family Orders mounted in diamonds. (Norman Parkinson)

The Queen Mother delights in meeting people, particularly children, as the pictures *overleaf* show. (Serge Lemoine)

The lovely studies of the Queen Mother on *pages 106 and 107* were taken by Norman Parkinson *left* and Cecil Beaton *right*.

The Queen abroad

No monarch in the history of the British Crown has met so many of her subjects as Queen Elizabeth II. She has achieved this by a series of jet-paced tours at home and in the Commonwealth countries.

She is not only Queen of the United Kingdom but also rules over, or has allegiance paid to her, by nearly twenty nations throughout the world, from Australia to Trinidad, and Canada to Tonga. Hardly any corner of the still vibrant Commonwealth has not been visited in the past twenty-five years at least once by her or a member of her family.

In addition, the Queen and Prince Philip have a new function – as well as cementing Commonwealth ties they are salesmen for Britain and British exports. Much of their work overseas is now linked with export promotion, a job they do well. During a highly successful tour of Japan in 1975 a West German diplomat said to one of his hosts at a British Embassy reception; "You've got the best salesmen in the world with your Queen and her husband…we can't match them."

A royal tour also helps either to build or to keep alive political links with other nations. The Queen paying a visit to a non-Commonwealth country is a gesture of friendship from Britain. The highly successful week the Queen and Prince Philip spent in West Germany during the early summer of 1978 was partly Britain letting the Common Market partner know it enjoyed having them as neighbours.

Not only does the Queen and the rest of her family find any visit to the United States enormously interesting, they also get a special thrill there because they are welcomed as America's own very special "royals". The Queen's links with the United States go back to the days when she went there for the first time with her husband shortly after their marriage. President Truman wrote to her father: "They went to the hearts of all the citizens."

Arranging a tour can sometimes take as long as two years. Before the formal invitations and acceptances are exchanged there are usually months of diplomatic discussions. When dates have been fixed an advance team is sent from Buckingham Palace about three months ahead. They check on security, the programme, pass on to the host nations matters of special interest to the royal guests, and even make sure that blood of the correct groups will be available. A confidential medical report is also sent to hospitals near the royal route so that a member of the party can be quickly and efficiently treated in an emergency.

Wherever the Queen goes in the world she does not drink the local water but insists on having only true-blue British Malvern water, the pure spring water that many people mix with whisky. The Queen takes dozens of bottles around the world with her, not to mix with alcohol, but because she does not wish to upset her tummy. She cannot afford to go down with an illness while touring.

Despite having her regular supply of Malvern water, the Queen still has to taste some strange foods when she is abroad. A local delicacy that might be considered a treat to the natives of one country is not often easy on the palate of one who is used to simple English cooking. Prince Charles reckons that he and his family have had to plough their way through so many strange concoctions that they all have cast-iron stomachs.

He and his relatives usually manage to keep expressions of approval and nod happily when being forced to taste in public some rare drink or food, but on at least one occasion Her Majesty could not prevent her natural digestive instincts from showing through.

This was in Kyoto, the fascinating ancient capital of Japan, during the royal tour of the country in 1975. The traditional tea ceremony is something the Japanese treasure and are proud of, though the product of this complicated piece of theatre can taste bitter and sickly to newcomers to the art.

A bowl of tea was offered to the Queen and Prince Philip by one of the best tea-makers in Japan. She accepted the greenish coloured, tepid liquid in the appropriate manner. This meant first of all turning the bowl round to admire the decorations around the side, and then taking a gulp of the contents. She looked, tasted – then almost retched as, with a grimace on her face, she handed the bowl back to the tea-maker and gave the prince a warning that he would have to suffer as well.

The Royal Yacht Britannia is frequently used at home and abroad as a floating Buckingham Palace. The Queen does not share her husband's love of the sea, however, and finds travelling on board distinctly upsetting. Because of this she prefers to fly to wherever the ship is anchored and usually only sails any distance on board when she is in calm waters.

Britannia, first launched in 1953, costs £10,000 a week to run while she is at sea, but half that amount when she is in dock. She has a permanent crew of 21 officers and 256 ratings, all of whom are entitled to wear the coveted insignia "Royal Yacht Service". There is no need for punishment for any misdemeanours among the crew – any trouble means a return to normal naval service.

When the Royal Family travels by air they usually go in one of the aircraft of the elite Queen's Flight, which is based at Benson in Oxfordshire. This distinctive fleet, painted bright red, includes three twin-engined Andover medium range airliners and two Wessex helicopters. They are manned and serviced by a 100-strong team and the operation costs around £1,000,000 a year to run.

Left. Her Majesty the Queen passing through an escort of warriors during her visit to the British Solomon Islands.

A smiling Queen *left* accepts a floral tribute in Finland, and is obviously pleased with her reception
above. (Les Wilson)
Overleaf. The Royal Yacht Brittania, pictured in Glenelg, South Australia.

A rather unusual method of transportation was provided for the Queen and Princess Anne when they were in the Cook Islands for the official opening of the new international airport on Rarotonga. They were carried *left* on wooden platforms on the shoulders of warriors.

In 1974 the Queen and Prince Philip, accompanied by Princess Anne and Captain Mark Phillips, spent three weeks touring New Zealand. As usual, they were warmly welcomed wherever they went. They are pictured *left centre* walking through the streets of Wellington and *left* singing hymns with local residents at a multi-denominational service. (Serge Lemoine)

Princess Anne was a very popular visitor to Bogota *above.* As she was leaving the Museum of Arts huge crowds massed, shouting "Viva la Bella Princessa"– a compliment greatly appreciated by Her Royal Highness.

An obviously happy Queen *above* with some of her young Commonwealth subjects during her visit to the British Solomon Islands.

No matter how packed her schedule, or how tired she may be, the Queen always has to appear smiling and interested, as she does here in Barbados *top left and below*, in Mexico *above and bottom left*, and in the Solomon Islands *left*.
(Serge Lemoine)

The attention of the Queen and Prince Philip is drawn to some aspect of the avenue of giant coconut trees they saw *above* during their visit to the National Trust Park in Barbados. (Serge Lemoine)

Overleaf. Her Majesty 'dotting the eyes of the dragon' during her visit to Hong Kong. (Colin Davey)

Many people throughout the world whose lives are such that they get very little opportunity to travel, particularly outside their own countries except, perhaps, once a year when they go on holiday, must consider that the most exciting part of being a member of the Royal Family would be the many tours they engage in, to all parts of the world. There are so many exotic places to be seen and so many interesting and famous people to meet; Presidents, film stars, leading sporting personalities and, of course, all the ordinary people who make other countries so fascinating. All this is true but what most of us may fail to realise is just how exacting Royal tours can be. Complicated shedules are worked out many weeks in advance and they have to be strictly adhered to, even to pacing out the distance between points of interest so that everything is prepared and the right people are waiting in the right places when the Queen herself walks the route.

Royal tours are also exhausting affairs. The simple fact is that there is one person whom everyone wants to meet and, if possible, speak to and the Queen is well aware of this and, however packed her schedule, she tries to ensure that as few people as possible are disappointed. She always appears smiling, interested and happy to meet the many people who are presented to her – something that most of us would surely find totally exhausting.

The pictures on these pages show just a small sample of the many tours the Royal Family has undertaken. *Top far left and near left bottom.* Her Majesty pictured during her 1972 tour of Yugoslavia. (Colin Davey)
Far left centre. Meeting Cub Scouts in Australia in 1977.

Near left centre. The Queen in France, escorted by President Pompidou. (R. Slade)
Far left bottom. The Queen and Prince Philip with members of the Japanese Royal Family, pictured when they visited Japan in 1975. (Colin Davey)
Near left top. Her Majesty with Prince Philip in Finland. (Les Wilson)
Above. The Queen in Mauritius during a tour she made in the year of her Silver Wedding anniversary. (Patrick Lichfield)
Top right and near left centre. The Royal visit to Barbados in Silver Jubilee Year. (Craig Burleigh)
Far right centre. Her Majesty talking to street traders in Hong Kong. (Colin Davey)
Right bottom. A few words exchanged with Arab dignitaries. (Jack Esten)
Far right bottom. Prince Charles in Kenya with Jomo Kenyatta and his wife. (Marion Kaplan)

Overleaf. The Queen, Prince Philip, Princess Anne and Captain Mark Phillips greeted by fantastically masked 'Mudmen' in New Guinea. (Serge Lemoine).

Her Majesty the Queen stepped ashore from the Royal Yacht Brittania, in Philadelphia, to begin her six day visit to the United States just two days after the start of the Bicentennial Celebrations. The itinerary concentrated heavily on the cities and states in the north-east which have the strongest connections with Britain. There were, of course, many official functions to attend, often with the President *these pages and overleaf.* (All pictures Colin Davey)

Extensive tours overseas are all part of the busy Royal programme.

In Mexico, during the first visit by a reigning British Monarch to that country, the Queen was pictured *top left* with President Echeverria, and *left* sheltering under an umbrella when rain interrupted an outdoor banquet *top right* held in her honour.

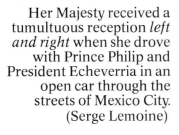

Her Majesty received a tumultuous reception *left and right* when she drove with Prince Philip and President Echeverria in an open car through the streets of Mexico City. (Serge Lemoine)

In November 1977 Her
Majesty the Queen, with
Prince Philip, flew to Ottawa
to commence a five day visit.
She carried out several
functions in and around the
city and was entertained at a
State Banquet, together with
Pierre Trudeau, the Prime
Minister of Canada, which
was held in her honour by
the Governor General. It was
a visit that the Queen greatly
enjoyed, particularly when
she was presented with a
horse by the Royal Canadian
Mounted Police *overleaf*.
The pictures on *pages 136
and 137* were also taken
during the Canadian visit.
(All pictures by Serge
Lemoine)

The Family at home

If the Queen, by an unlikely chance, was suffering from overcrowding at Buckingham Palace, she can still turn for space to a total of twenty royal homes and palaces in Britain. Including the recently acquired country houses of Prince Charles and Princess Anne, that is the number of residences linked with the sovereign.

There are palaces which have not had a member of the ruling family in for centuries but are part of the nation's heritage. There are also buildings, large and small, which the family do not just regard as part of the trappings of their function but as homes.

The royal homes and palaces used regularly are: Buckingham Palace, Kensington Palace and Clarence House in London; Windsor Castle, Royal Lodge, Windsor, and Fort Belvedere, Windsor; Sandringham House in Norfolk; Chevening House in Kent; Gatcombe Park in Gloucestershire; the Palace of Holyroodhouse, Edinburgh; Glamis Castle in Angus; Balmoral Castle and Birkhall in Aberdeenshire; and the Castle of Mey in Caithness.

Palaces associated with the throne but not used by the sovereign these days in London are: The Palace of Westminster (the Houses of Commons and Lords); Westminster Hall; Lancaster House; Marlborough House; St. James's Palace and the Tower of London.

Buckingham Palace originally belonged to the Dukes of Buckingham until the property was bought by George III for £21,000 in 1762. It was smaller then, and most of what we see today was built in the hundred years following the Crown acquisition.

George III and his wife, Queen Charlotte, purchased it originally as a retreat from nearby St. James's Palace, which was then the official home of the sovereign. It still is, to some degree, because ambassadors are accredited to the "Court of St. James"…although they present their credentials at Buckingham Palace.

George and Charlotte regarded it as a family home, where they could escape to from the affairs of State, and it was not until George IV came to the throne that the decision was made to turn it into a grand palace. That great Regency architect John Nash was called in to organise the transformation, but the king died before it was ready for occupation. So did his successor, younger brother King William IV. The first monarch to use Buckingham Palace as a permanent official home was Queen Victoria, who moved her court into the building in 1837. It has become not just a London home for the Queen and her family, but also a busy office block – a Government department administering Crown affairs.

It must have the most photographed balcony in the world. That raised terrace above the main entrance is traditionally used by a sovereign to appear before the crowds at times of major celebrations. Victories, coronations, weddings and births have all been marked by the familiar line-up of royal hand wavers looking down on the revellers below.

Members of the public can now get a glimpse of some of the marbled and scarlet decor inside by visiting the art exhibition in the Queen's Gallery. This used to be the private chapel where royal babies were christened and monarchs and their families and staff occasionally worshipped. Only a small part of the chapel remains – the rest was destroyed by bombs in the Second World War. (During that war Buckingham Palace was damaged nine times by bombs, or the forerunner of today's guided missiles, the flying bombs).

The Queen decided that the old chapel should be rebuilt as an art gallery where her private collection could be put on display. The work was completed in time for opening in 1962. All the profits from visitors to the gallery, as well as income from the days when the public are allowed around Sandringham, Windsor Castle and Balmoral, are given to charities.

Buckingham Palace and Windsor Castle now belong to the nation, but Balmoral and Sandringham, used by the family nearly three months of each year, are among the private estates of the Queen.

Balmoral and nearby Birkhall, which is the Queen Mother's favourite retreat, are places where they can relax as a group easier than anywhere else. They can move around the heathered countryside without being bothered too much by sightseers and most of the villagers are familiar old faces to them. In Scotland they become "lairds", wearing kilts of Royal Stuart tartan or the special Balmoral tartan which is a weave of black, red, grey and lavender.

Sandringham consists of 20,000 acres of windy agricultural land in north Norfolk, where the family gathers for a month after spending Christmas at Windsor Castle. It is used as a place to invite friends from London for informal country weekends, and as a centre for Prince Philip and Prince Charles when they organise their shooting parties.

Windsor Castle is regarded mainly as a weekend home, although it has one troublesome problem… the noise from aircraft taking off from nearby Heathrow, one of the world's busiest airports.

Gatcombe Park, the new Gloucestershire home of Princess Anne and Captain Mark Phillips, is a 730-acre estate which the Queen bought for her daughter in 1976. The cost is reputed to have been three-quarters-of-a-million pounds and more money has been spent on renovations, repairs and providing quarters and training facilities for horses. Sheltered among the Cotswold Hills, it has 530 acres of farmland and 200 acres of woods, plus a lake stocked with trout.

Prince Charles's home, Chevening, near Sevenoaks in Kent, is a 250-year-old mansion among 3,000 acres of park and woodland. It has 24 acres of landscaped gardens and a four acre lake. It was the home of generations of the Earls Stanhope, a family that devoted itself to public service. When the seventh earl died without an heir in 1967 he left it to the nation, hoping that Charles would take up the offer. He also left £250,000 for the repair and maintenance of the house.

A modern touch that Charles has brought to the Eighteenth Century atmosphere is hi-fi music. He has loudspeakers in every room.

The Queen, the Queen Mother and Prince Andrew *above* relaxing on a Sunday morning when they attended the veterinary inspection at the Badminton Horse Trials. (Serge Lemoine)

The Royal Family are great followers of equestrian events and, when they are not able to take part, they thoroughly enjoy watching, whatever the weather, as the pictures *right* show. (Serge Lemoine)

On her 25th wedding anniversary the Queen was pictured *overleaf* with her family, from left to right: Princess Margaret, Lord Snowdon, Lady Sarah Armstrong-Jones, Duchess of Kent–holding her son Lord Nicholas Windsor, Duke of Kent, the Queen Mother, Prince Michael of Kent, Viscount Linley, Prince Philip, the Queen, Earl of St Andrews–the Duke of Kent's eldest son, Prince Charles, Prince Edward and Lady Helen Windsor–the Duke of Kent's daughter –seated on floor, Princess Anne, Prince Andrew, Marina Ogilvy– daughter of Princess Alexandra, Hon. Angus Ogilvy, Princess Alexandra, James Ogilvy. (Patrick Lichfield)

The importance that the Royal Family places on the 'family' side of their lives cannot be too highly stressed. Because of their unique position it is difficult for them to go outside their own close circle and they are therefore a very self sustaining group of people. It would also be very difficult for any of them to relax completely other than with their own relatives and relaxation is, as everyone knows, an extremely important part of anyone's life. The picture *top left* shows the Queen with her immediate family at the time of her Silver Wedding. With her are Prince Philip, Prince Charles, Princess Anne, Prince Andrew and Prince Edward at Balmoral. (Patrick Lichfield)

Prince Charles is shown *right* with his sister, Princess Anne in Australia. *Far left centre.* Princess Margaret's daughter, Lady Sarah Armstrong-Jones. *Near left centre.* Lady Helen Windsor, the Duke of Kent's daughter. Prince Andrew is shown *far left, bottom* and Prince Edward *bottom centre.* The Queen and her two youngest sons, the Princes Andrew and Edward are pictured together with Prince Philip *below.* (Roger Garwood, Peter Grugeon)

Father, son and daughter in serious mood *left, far left, and centre left, below.* Prince Philip was about to enter the dressage ring with his carriage and four at the Royal Windsor Horse Show and Prince Charles was pictured at the opening of the Prince of Wales Hospital in Brisbane, Australia. Princess Anne had let her long, blonde hair down when she was photographed at the Badminton Horse Trials and Captain Mark Phillips *centre left* was very happy to share a joke with other competitors.

A smiling Princess Anne photographed during a visit to a farm in Columbia *near right, top,* and a windswept Princess Alexandra with her husband Angus Ogilvy *below left.*

Princess Anne is pictured with her father and young brother *top right,* at a time when she was too young to compete in major show-jumping events and had to be content to watch. (Serge Lemoine)

The Queen Mother is always a great favourite wherever she goes. She is shown *far left, bottom* being escorted round an agricultural show in London by Massey Ferguson's former Managing Director, Mr William Beath.

146

Prince Philip practising
with his carriage and four
in the grounds of Windsor
Castle *right*.

The Prince of Wales *below*
giving an animated
description of some
obviously humorous event
to the Duchess of Kent.

Overleaf. Prince Philip
and Princess Anne tending
the barbecue at Balmoral.
(Patrick Lichfield)

A typical crowd scene *left* at Ascot as Her Majesty returns to her box from the paddock, where she had been inspecting the runners. The Queen and other members of the Royal Family are present every day during Ascot week, which is the highlight of the London Season. In addition to the spectacle, Ascot offers some of the finest and most important racing of the year.

The Derby, which takes place on Epsom Downs, is another important race regularly attended by the Queen *below and all facing pictures*. She watches the racing from the Royal Box *below centre* and assesses the entries in the paddock *right and far right*. (Serge Lemoine)

There were formal portraits taken to commemorate the Queen and Prince Philip's Silver Wedding, as well as the charming outdoor photographs shown here and *overleaf.* All three photographs were taken at Balmoral, the Queen's much-loved Scottish home, and show *left* Prince Philip fly-fishing and *below* Her Majesty riding her horse Cossack in the grounds of Balmoral Castle, which can be seen in the background. The lovely picture of the Queen *right* sitting by a waterfall in the castle grounds features two of her corgis – Tiny is on Her Majesty's knee and Brush is at her feet. (All pictures by Patrick Lichfield)

Whenever the Queen is able to relax in the country it is almost certain that there will be animals with her, particularly dogs and horses. (Patrick Lichfield)

Her Majesty is pictured *below* at the Palace of Holyroodhouse. (Alex Wilson)

Her Majesty planting a tree *top left* at Camperdown Park, Dundee, and attending a Jubilee show in Glasgow *centre left, above*. She is pictured *above* when she arrived at North Hobart Oval to attend the Tasmania Military Tattoo.

The Queen Mother with Prince Philip *left* in Edinburgh, and with Princess Margaret *top right*.

A formal photograph *below* taken at Holyroodhouse during the King of Sweden's visit.

The Queen in Oxford in March 1976 *right*, and Prince Charles *below right* on board his first command, HMS Bronington.

A happy Queen *above* prepares to present the prizes on the final day of the Badminton Horse Trials. (Serge Lemoine)

Her Majesty always seems to enjoy her visits to Scotland, whether she is at Balmoral, the Palace of Holyroodhouse, attending funtions or enjoying the unique spectacle of the Braemar Games which features events that are rarely seen, if ever, anywhere else in the world. (Colin Davey, Alex Wilson, Lesley Wilson)

It is surprising that the Queen ever finds time for all the photographs that are taken of her, so busy is her schedule. Even when relaxing in the country she still manages to spare some time for photographers, but outdoor shots, particularly unposed 'candids' are very little problem compared to the time that has to be spent on arranging and lighting many of the indoor sessions *left, right and far right*. (Peter Grugeon)

Nowadays there is far more interest in seeing the Royal Family 'doing something', such as sorting their mail, *below*.

Both the charming outdoor studies *overleaf* were taken at Balmoral. (Patrick Lichfield)

Left, above right, far right top, and near right, bottom. On the 6th June, in Silver Jubilee Year, Her Majesty the Queen lit a special Jubilee bonfire in Windsor Great Park which was the signal for a chain of similar bonfires to be lit over the length and breadth of the country, heralding the start of the Jubilee celebrations.

Fireworks, *far right,* pattern the sky over the Thames as part of the Silver Jubilee celebrations.

Above The Queen, wearing a tweed coat and scarf, smiles while watching her husband compete in a carriage-driving competition in Windsor Great Park.

Centre right On her way to present prizes at the Windsor Horse Show, the Queen wears a green coat and matching bonnet. (Serge Lemoine)

There were several members of the Royal Family present at 1975's 'Wedding of the Year' when Lord Patrick Lichfield married Lady Leonora Grosvenor *overleaf.* (Peter Kain)

Princess Margaret

The lovely photographs of Princess Margaret *above and right* were both taken in 1953.

The Throne Room of Buckingham Palace was the setting for the photograph *overleaf* of the family group, taken after Princess Margaret and Anthony Armstrong-Jones' wedding ceremony.

A charming study *right* of
Princess Margaret, her
husband Lord Snowdon and
their two children Viscount
Linley – on his father's
shoulders, and Lady Sarah
Armstrong-Jones – in her
mother's arms.

Princess Margaret, Countess
of Snowdon, pictured in 1961
with her first child David,
Viscount Linley. The picture
was taken by the Princess's
husband Lord Snowdon.
The Princess photographed
in the gardens of Kensington
Palace in 1965 *below* and
with her son, Viscount Linley,
below right. (Cecil Beaton)

The marriage that had started with such fairy tale promise in May 1960 was virtually over by the time Princess Margaret and her husband decided to separate in 1976 and, in fact, they were divorced two years later, in 1978. The break-up of a marriage can never be anything other than a tragedy, particularly when there are children involved, but when it has to happen in the full glare of publicity then the difficulties must be enormous.

Left. The Princess photographed in 1975. (Norman Parkinson)
Right. Princess Margaret with her children, Viscount Linley and Lady Sarah Armstrong-Jones in 1973 (Patrick Lichfield) and in 1975 *below.* (Norman Parkinson) Two more studies of the Princess and her childrem are shown *overleaf.* (Norman Parkinson)

Prince Charles

Prince Charles, the twenty-first Prince of Wales, has set himself one task above all others before he becomes King. He wishes to learn at first hand as much as possible about the people he will govern. He also wants to experience as much of life as he can before the crown curbs his adventurous spirit.

As Prince of Wales he is the latest in a line that includes Edward, the warrior Black Prince of the fourteenth century, the much-married Henry the Eighth, Queen Victoria's son, the fun-loving Edward VII, and the late Duke of Windsor.

His full title is His Royal Highness the Prince Charles Philip Arthur George, Prince of Wales and Earl of Chester, Duke of Cornwall and Rothesay, Earl of Carrick and Baron of Renfrew, Lord of the Isles and Great Steward of Scotland, Knight of The Garter.

The titles Prince of Wales and Earl of Chester are traditionally associated with a male heir apparent of a reigning monarch. On the death of a Prince of Wales and Earl of Chester they do not pass on to his son – they must be recreated with each reign. Cornwall and the five Scottish titles came to Charles as eldest son of the sovereign, from the moment the Queen ascended to the throne. Edward III created his son Duke of Cornwall in 1337 making it clear that the title should descend to the eldest sons of English rulers forever. The Scottish titles come from the fourteenth century. James VI of Scotland brought them with him when he became James I of England following the death of the first Queen Elizabeth. Charles holds them as heir to the old kingdom of Scotland.

Unlike most of his predecessors, Charles devotes a large part of his time to Wales and its affairs. Whether it be Welsh industry, art, music or the national rite of rugby, he gets involved.

When the Queen decided Charles should take up the title of Prince of Wales, she was determined that he should have more than just a formal link with the principality. He learned the Welsh language – the first English Prince of Wales to do so – and he went to the University College of Wales, Aberystwyth, to absorb Welsh culture. The Welsh language is not one of the easiest to learn and in fact is spoken by less than half of the population. Yet in a few months Charles mastered enough of it not only to give his investiture speech in Welsh, but also to hold a conversation in the tongue.

His popularity both at home and abroad was best summed up at his investiture as Prince of Wales in July 1969, when the Mayor of Caernarvon said "Look at him, he's the ace in the royal pack!"

Charles feels that he can make a useful contribution to the life of the monarchy and the country... such as the work he did organising Jubilee Year, his interest in young people and the efforts he makes on behalf of Wales. He has, for instance, helped to attract more industry to the area.

Realising that he is very different from the ordinary people, Charles goes to great lengths to bring himself closer to those who will, one day, be his subjects.

Charles' spirit of adventure is such that there seems to be few things he has not tried. In the Canadian Arctic he donned a rubber suit and spent more than half an hour underneath the ice pack – in temperatures that were four degrees below that needed to make ice in a refrigerator.

When he was recently appointed Colonel-in-Chief of the Parachute Regiment, he was not content to accept it as merely an honorary title. He wanted to be able to wear the wings because he had earned them. "If I'm going to be the colonel, I'll do it properly", he said. He therefore joined other members of the regiment in a series of jumps that brought him up to combat standard. Only then would he stitch on his uniform the coveted insignia of a paratrooper. Explaining his taste for danger, he says: "It tends to make you appreciate life that much more and really to want to live it to the fullest."

The prince has always had a bubbling sense of humour – ever since childhood. "I enjoy making people laugh," he says. "It's very useful for getting people to listen to what you are saying". Both he and Andrew like the weird comedy style of Peter Sellers and the Goons. At one very stiff regimental dinner, he sang the gibberish song made famous by Sellers, the "Ying-Tong" song. Keeping a straight face, he repeated over and over again the verse: "Ying-Tong, Ying-Tong, Ying-Tong, Ying-Tong, Tiddle-I-Po." It certainly broke the ice around the mess table.

Soldiers in his Royal Regiment of Wales grumbled that, because they did not speak any German, they were having trouble meeting the local girls where they were stationed at Osnabruck. A few days later Charles sent them two light-hearted sheets of German-English phrases with a vocabulary limited to the pursuit of women.

At a charity cricket match he once went out to bat mounted on a pony and carrying a polo stick. When everyone was wearing name tags at a Royal Air Force dinner Charles' label said: "Watch this space".

He is gradually taking from his parents much of the burden of public appearances, official duties, and foreign touring, adopting a sort of vice-presidential role. His interests are so great that he is the president or patron of more than 140 organisations and societies and colonel-in-chief of ten regiments. The activities in which he gets involved range from preserving the natural beauty of Wales to blowing the trumpet for British industry.

Charles knows that he is likely to be King in a period of social, economic and political changes, but he has been carefully groomed for the task. "I worry sometimes about the future," he once said, "but I think that if one can preserve one's sense of humour, adaptive qualities and perhaps help to calm things down...to provide a stable appearance and approach to things, a steadying influence – all will be well."

As to his ever-interesting marriage prospects, he has answered on at least one occasion to endless questions on the subject: "This is awfully difficult, because you have to remember that when you marry in my position you are going to marry someone who is perhaps one day going to be Queen".

There are, and indeed have to be, many sides to the life of Prince Charles. His main preoccupation, of course, must be that of preparing himself for his eventual role as King and, to that end, he was invested as Prince of Wales *above, top and right* by Her Majesty the Queen at Caernarvon Castle in 1969. Away from the pomp of such duties, however, the Prince loves the outdoor life, whether it be attending a sporting event at Cowdray Park *left centre* or simply enjoying the fresh air of Balmoral *top left and far left centre*. (Godfrey Argent, Patrick Lichfield, Norman Parkinson)

A relaxed and sun-tanned Prince Charles *above left* in Coolangatta, Australia, and rather less relaxed *left* as he takes the reins of a stage-coach in Ballarat, also in Australia.

The Prince of Wales in Ghana *above and top* where he attended a gathering of Ashanti Chiefs, several of whom were introduced to him *right*. (Serge Lemoine)

Prince Charles' popularity seems to increase with each passing year. As the future King his duties are numerous and varied and he is constantly required to travel, both in Britain and abroad. Whatever his duties, however, and no matter how arduous his schedules he always seems to find time to meet a variety of people and to appear relaxed and happy in their company – and perhaps this is the secret of his popularity.
(Serge Lemoine)

A Prince, particularly the heir apparent, is required to fill a multitude of roles. These include such duties as presiding over the passing-out parade of Ghanaian Army cadets and then posing for a formal picture with them *top left*, and watching a Durbar – a gathering of Ashanti Chiefs – *left*. In complete contrast, though no less formal in its way, Prince Charles was presented with full Red Indian dress in Canada and he managed to wear the unfamiliar clothes with considerable dignity *above and overleaf*. (Serge Lemoine)

Page 192 (45mm)
Jubilee Year was, besides being a very happy year for Her Majesty the Queen and her family, an extremely busy one. In particular, the weeks leading up to Jubilee Day, and the weeks after, were crammed with engagements. Jubilee Day was in June and the Trooping the Colour Ceremony always takes place in that month and it was at the end of a very busy week that Prince Charles reviewed, on a Sunday morning, the veterans of the Royal British Legion on Horse Guards Parade. The occasion was a solemn one with the veterans, men and women, proudly carrying their flags and parading in front of the Prince of Wales. (All pictures by Serge Lemoine)

Overleaf. A group of beautiful girls from the Ivory Coast, their dresses decorated with Prince Charles' picture, await his arrival at the airport in Ghana. (Serge Lemoine)

One thing that can most certainly be said of Prince Charles is that he is game to try his hand at practically anything. As the future King he may, if he wishes, serve in all three branches of the armed services. He has already shown his ability as a pilot and he is pictured *top right* in February 1976, taking command of HMS Bronington, a 360 ton minehunter.

The Prince does not, however, confine his activities only to those that might be expected of him. He was happy to dance with a local beauty *top left* in Fiji; he donned protective gear during a visit to a logging plant in Tasmania *top centre*, is an accomplished polo player *above and far left centre*, and he even made a dive of some sixty feet deep into the freezing waters under the ice-cap at Resolute Bay in the Arctic, to visit an undersea research laboratory. (Serge Lemoine)

In November of Jubilee Year, 1977, Prince Charles made a fifteen day visit to the United States which started in Chicago and ended in the lovely city of San Francisco. During his tour the Prince visited Texas and was entertained by Mrs Anne Armstrong, the former United States Ambassador to London, and her husband, with whom he is pictured *left*. He also, whilst on their ranch, had a chance to enjoy a game of polo *bottom right*.

One of the highlights of his trip was a visit to the Houston Space Centre, where he had an opportunity to try out a moon landing vehicle *right* and to see other exhibits connected with the space programme *below*. (All pictures by Serge Lemoine)

199

Prince Charles was made a local Chief whilst in Ghana and he appeared to enjoy wearing his new robes of office *above*. (Serge Lemoine)

Prince Andrew *right* travelled to Northern Ireland to join the Queen on her last official visit during her Silver Jubilee tour of the United Kingdom. (Serge Lemoine)

Princess Anne

A young wife and mother, just beginning to lay the foundations of a home and family, Princess Anne still finds time for involvement in charity work, her riding career and the demands of public life.

Being the only girl in the Queen's family Anne has to cope with more than usual pressures and, in addition to being herself, she has always had to remember her position as a member of the Royal Family. It was not easy merely to grow up, fall in love and have children like anyone else and yet Anne has coped with it all superbly, never forgetting the role she has to play.

The admiration for the princess and her husband, Captain Mark Phillips, that exists throughout the world was best demonstrated one balmy evening at the airport on the Caribbean island of Barbados when the couple flew in to begin their honeymoon. Three of the best calypso bands in the West Indies had rehearsed a selection of music to greet them and thousands of happy islanders packed the airport perimeter and reception area shouting their good wishes and carrying banners with such slogans as "Have a good time Anne baby!" or "Well done Mark!"

The route from the airport to the capital and main port, Bridgetown, was lined with more flag and banner-waving crowds – all pleased to see at last the Queen's daughter they had heard so much about.

This is the sort of reception, though sometimes less boisterous, that the princess receives wherever she goes, at home or abroad.

Among the many fund-raising operations with which she is associated, the one closest to her main interest is the Riding for the Disabled Association. Apart from lending her name to appeals and making speeches on its behalf as patron, she frequently visits tiny riding schools dotted around Britain to encourage physically handicapped children to train in horsemanship.

Anne and Mark moved into their new home, Gatcombe Park in the Cotswolds, at the time of the birth of their first baby in November 1977. Both she and her husband were against giving the child a title, although he is fifth in line to the throne. With a suitably democratic touch, he remained Master Peter Mark Andrew Phillips, the first grandchild of the Queen and the first so high in the royal line to be born a commoner in more than 500 years.

Young Master Phillips, who cried throughout his christening in the Music Room of Buckingham Palace, was given his first name after his paternal grandfather, the second name followed that of his father and Andrew is not only the name of one of his uncles, but it is also that of Prince Philip's father, the late Prince Andrew of Greece.

The pictures *left and above* of Princess Anne were taken on the occasion of her twenty-first birthday in 1971. (Norman Parkinson)
A birthday two years later saw the publication of the pictures *overleaf* of the Princess. (Patrick Lichfield)

Princess Anne and Captain Mark Phillips were married in 1973 and, during that year, there were many photographs of the happy couple. The photographs on these pages were all taken in the grounds of Frogmore House which provided some particularly attractive locations in which to photograph the young Princess and her cavalry officer. In the picture *right* Captain Phillips is shown wearing the No. 1 Dress uniform of his regiment. (All pictures by Norman Parkinson)

Before entering the arena to take part in a dressage event Princess Anne discusses one of the finer points of the competition with, or perhaps seeks the advice of, her husband Captain Mark Phillips *top left.* The Princess greatly enjoys taking part in competitions as is clear from her happy expression *above, and bottom left.*

On Sunday, the last day of the Badminton Horse Trials, Princess Margaret and her daughter, Lady Sarah Armstrong-Jones, *top centre* walk to Badminton church to attend morning service.

Prince Philip has chosen carriage and four driving *far right, centre* as a sport to replace polo. A considerable amount of skill, and strong nerves, are required to control a lively team. The Prince is pictured *centre left* taking part in an obstacle race at Windsor. (Serge Lemoine)

Determinedly walking the course *top right* before the competition at the Burghley European Championships, are Princess Anne, Captain Mark Phillips, and their trainer Mrs Alison Oliver.

Princess Margaret *below* takes her daughter, Lady Sarah Armstrong-Jones, to watch Prince Philip compete, with his carriage and four, in an event in the Windsor Horse Show. (Serge Lemoine)

Sailing is another sport that Princess Anne enjoys. While visiting West Berlin she took the opportunity to take a closer look at the East Sector by sailing *right* on a lake dividing the city. (Serge Lemoine)

All the Royal family are interested in photography and Princess Anne *left* is no exception.

The photographs *below and below right* were taken at Oak Grove House, Sandhurst, which was, at the time, the home of Princess Anne and Captain Mark Phillips. In the picture below the Princess is shown with Florence, her young cocker spaniel, and in the picture below right with her black labrador Moriarty, watching horse trials.
(R. Slade, Srdja Djukanovic, Les Wilson)

Princess Anne is shown *far left* relaxing with her horse Goodwill before a competition in Windsor Great Park, and being congratulated *left* by Captain Mark Phillips after completing a faultless round in the cross-country event at the European Championships in West Germany. Apart from the picture *above* of her husband in the unfamiliar role of spectator, all the other pictures show the Princess enjoying various aspects of her favourite sport. (Serge Lemoine)

Photographed in the Crimson
Drawing Room at Windsor
Castle, Princess Anne is
shown *left* wearing a
champagne lace dress,
diamond tiara, diamond
necklace, diamond earrings
and sapphire and diamond
engagement ring. Captain
Mark Phillips is wearing the
No.1 Dress uniform of his
regiment.

In the pictures on this page,
which were released only a
week or so before the
wedding, the Princess is
wearing a black silk shirt and
trousers with a black and
gold caftan. Captain Phillips
is in the Mess Kit of his
regiment.

The two photographs
overleaf feature Princess
Anne and Captain Mark
Phillips *left* and the Princess
alone, wearing white furs
right. (All pictures by
Norman Parkinson)

The Princess and Captain Mark Phillips, of the Queen's Dragoon Guards, pictured *above and on page 222* in the Long Gallery at Windsor Castle. (Norman Parkinson)
The happy couple *right and on page 223* in Buckingham Palace on their wedding day, November 14th 1973. (Norman Parkinson)
The magnificent scene in Westminster Abbey *overleaf* taken during the wedding of Princess Anne and Captain Mark Phillips. (Serge Lemoine)

One of the happiest Royal events of recent years was the engagement and subsequent marriage of Princess Anne to Captain Mark Phillips. Following the announcement of their engagement they were seldom out of the headlines and pictures of them appeared almost daily, until well after they returned from their honeymoon. Whether in this country or abroad, attending premieres or exchanging their first kiss in public, the photographers were always there, preserving each moment for posterity. (All pictures on these pages and overleaf by Serge Lemoine)

Princess Anne is a much-travelled member of the Royal Family. A keen and accomplished horse-woman, she found herself on a rather unusual mount – a donkey – *left* when she went trekking in Ethiopia.

A charming smile from the Princess *above* when she attended a garden party in Quito, Ecuador.

An obviously very relaxed Prince Philip *top left* comments on an athletic event to Princess Anne when they watched the Commonwealth Games in Christchurch, New Zealand.

Large-brimmed hats can cause problems for photographers due to the heavy shadows they cast, but this particular picture *right*, taken when Princess Anne attended the opening ceremony of the international airport in Raratonga, in the Cook Islands, proves the exception to the rule. (Serge Lemoine)

In 1961 Prince Edward, the Duke of Kent, married the lovely Katherine Worsley. They have three children: the Earl of St Andrews, who was born in June 1962, Lady Helen Windsor, born in April 1964 and Lord Nicholas Windsor, who arrived in July 1970. The pictures of the Duke and Duchess *top left and right* were taken in 1972. (Barry Lategan)

The photographs of the Duchess *above*, the Duke and Duchess with Lord Nicholas *left*, and both the pictures *overleaf* were taken at the family's country home – Anmer Hall, which is near King's Lynn in Norfolk. (Norman Parkinson)

Before moving to Anmer Hall, the Duke of Kent and his family lived at Coppins, at Iver in Buckinghamshire, which is where the photograph on *pages 234 and 235* was taken. (Tom Hustler)

The Duke and Duchess of Kent

Princess Alexandra's family

The study *left* was the first colour picture taken of Princess Alexandra with her son,
James Robert Bruce, who was born in February 1964. (Cecil Beaton)

Princess Alexandra, the Queen's cousin, married Angus Ogilvy in 1963 and they made their home at Thatched House Lodge in Richmond Park, near London, where all the photographs on these pages and *overleaf* were taken. The Ogilvy's have two children, James Robert Bruce, born in 1964, and Marina Victoria Alexandra, 1966. (Picture left by Cecil Beaton, all others by Norman Parkinson)

The Duke and Duchess of Gloucester

Prince Richard, Duke of Gloucester, and the Duchess are the subjects of the two beautiful photographs *above and left* which were taken at Barnwell Manor, the family home in Northamptonshire. (Norman Parkinson)

Prince Richard, the younger son of the Duke and Duchess of Gloucester, married Birgitte van Deurs, the daughter of a prominent Danish lawyer, in July 1972. In the photograph taken after the ceremony *overleaf* may be seen some of the many royal guests, including Princess Margaret, Prince Charles and the Queen Mother. (Tom Hustler)

Prince Richard and his bride cutting their wedding cake *left* and with their first child – Alexander Patrick Gregers Richard, Earl of Ulster *top right, centre right and right* on the occasion of his christening. (Tom Hustler, Norman Parkinson, Tim Jenkins)

Her Majesty the Queen's Silver Jubilee visits started on the island of Tonga in February 1977. On landing on the island they were greeted by His Majesty King Taufa'ahau Tupou IV, GCVO, KCMG, KBE, and Her Majesty Queen Halaevalu Maca'aho.

The Queen is pictured *above* in happy, smiling mood on the lawn of the Tongan Royal Palace.

The King and Queen of Tonga welcoming Her Majesty and Prince Philip *overleaf* as they disembark from the Royal Yacht Brittania at Nuku'alofa.

In Fiji the Queen and Prince Philip toured the sports ground at Labasa *above left* and attended a garden party, where they watched Fijian and Indian dancers, some of whom are shown *left*. (All pictures: Serge Lemoine).

Silver Jubilee Year

uring 1977 the whole world joined in the celebration of the Queen's Silver Jubilee – the twenty-fifth anniversary of her accession to the throne.

Millions of people came to Britain from all parts of the globe to witness or take part in the festivities. Those who could not be there cabled good wishes or sent letters in almost every known language.

The Queen and her family made special efforts, however, to greet the Commonwealth with fast, exhausting tours overseas.

The beginning of that incredible year was a six-week long visit by Her Majesty and Prince Philip to the South Pacific, New Zealand and Australia.

After a brief stop in Samoa to board the royal yacht Britannia they spent a few days in Tonga and Fiji. In Tonga they were greeted by the giant, 28-stone king, His Majesty Taufa'ahau Tupou IV, who treated them to a feast of roast wild pigs, lobsters and exotic fruits.

One of the highlights of the visit to Fiji was the greeting out at sea off Suva harbour by hundreds of small boats, and the boarding of the Britannia by local chiefs in colourful, warrior-like costumes.

Warriors of another kind met the royal party at the start of their two weeks in New Zealand. Maoris massed in front of them with their frightening war chants and performed a mock battle.

The Queen's fondness for 'walkabouts' – just wandering among the people – proved very successful in bringing her closer to delighted crowds. In one of her speeches she even tried speaking a little Maori.

During Jubilee Year the Queen received many thousands of gifts, from rich and poor, Governments and business organisations, but few gave her as much pleasure as the horse she was given at a Parliamentary reception in Canberra when her Australian journey began. Visibly pleased, she told the Australians: "I thank you all for this imaginative and exciting jubilee gift".

In two very hectic weeks the royal pair went to every state in Australia, going out of their way to try to meet as many people as possible – not just the officials at banquets and formal lunches, but the children and their parents lining the streets.

The Queen was barely back in Britain at the end of March before she set out on a back-breaking four months of visits and ceremonial duties.

This included reviewing the three services, especially the Royal Navy, whose ships were joined by vessels from other nations in a spectacular display of sea power off Spithead in the Solent.

The last time so many warships had gathered in ranks for Her Majesty was twenty-four years earlier, in the same anchorage, after her coronation. The ships this time were smaller, but with modern weapons the firepower was greater.

Not to be outdone, the Royal Air Force put on a dramatic fly-past of jet fighters and bombers at their Finningley base in Nottinghamshire which ended with twenty-two aircraft swooping over in formation in the shape of a '25'.

To receive the Army's tribute the Queen and the Prince went to West Germany, where the Rhine Army roared past in tanks, armoured troop carriers and helicopters.

On the eve of the official Jubilee Day – June 7th – the whole country was, literally, set alight. The Queen put a flame to a bonfire near her home at Windsor Great Park which sparked off a chain that spread the length and breadth of Britain.

The following day, watched by millions throughout the world on television, one of the greatest processions through London since the coronation took place. The Queen, with Prince Philip, drove in the 216-year old Golden State Coach from Buckingham Palace two miles through the centre of London to St. Paul's Cathedral for a service of thanksgiving.

Lining the route were military bands and thousands of troops, and the streets were packed with nearly a hundred thousand rainsoaked flag wavers from all over the world, many of whom had camped overnight in the rain.

Leading the mile long procession was a troop of scarlet-clad Royal Canadian Mounted Police, while behind them were coaches and open carriages carrying the Royal Family and Statesmen.

All the family except one – Prince Charles, who, looking dashing in the tall bearskin and crimson jacket of a colonel-in-chief of the Welsh Guards, rode as an escort alongside his mother and father on a sleek black horse that had just been given to him by the Mounties. A horse he nearly fell off at St. Paul's, because someone had put the dismounting block on television later, it wasn't as disastrous as I had thought", said Charles.

The sun came out, at last, by the end of the cathedral service, and the Queen and Philip walked through the streets of the City of London to the fifteenth century Guildhall for a banquet.

In one of the most significant speeches of her reign the Queen said at the Guildhall: "When I was 21, I pledged my life to the service of our people and I asked for God's help to make good that vow. Although that vow was made in my salad days, when I was green in judgement, I do not regret nor retract one word of it."

That tumultuous day ended with one of the biggest firework displays ever seen along the shores of the Thames. All the multi-coloured rockets were cleverly matched to music by Handel relayed over loudspeakers.

The Queen achieved two firsts during August…her first trip in a helicopter, which was necessary for security reasons, and her first visit to Northern Ireland since the outbreak of the sectarian fighting. She and Philip also took along Prince Andrew, as if to let the troubled population know that the Royal Family had not forgotten them.

In farewell words of encouragement she said: "I look forward to the day when we may return to enjoy with the people of Northern Ireland some of the better and happier times so long awaited and so richly deserved."

At the end of the summer Her Majesty finished her jubilee tours with a visit to Canada.

On many of her official visits overseas, the Queen uses the Royal Yacht Brittania as a temporary residence. This provides her with what is, effectively, British territory on which she can receive visiting dignitaries and which also serves as the nerve centre of the Monarchy, as well as providing accommodation and offices – albeit sometimes rather cramped – for all the various officials, policemen, pages, doctors, secretaries and servants who accompany Her Majesty. Such trips require an enormous amount of organization and an equally impressive amount of luggage. (Serge Lemoine)

Wearing a traditional Maori cape presented to her when she toured New Zealand during Silver Jubilee Year, Her Majesty the Queen accepts the Maori challenge *above* which allows her, by tradition, to enter their lands. Later, she watched dancers from the Polynesian Islands *bottom left* and walked among the crowds who had come to see her and to offer her their greetings.

The Queen smiles happily during another of her walkabouts in New Zealand *right and overleaf*. (All pictures: Serge Lemoine).

The pictures *left and above* were taken during walkabouts in New Zealand. The walkabouts were arranged following the express wish of Her Majesty to meet as many people as possible during her stay. (Serge Lemoine).

The Queen was obviously delighted with the reception she received in New Zealand and even the weather that prevailed during her short stop at Blenheim *right* did nothing to dampen her pleasure.

Her Majesty preparing to deliver her speech *overleaf* at the opening of a new session of Parliament in Wellington, New Zealand. (All pictures: Serge Lemoine).

During her tours abroad, both in Jubilee Year and before, the Queen has met with various customs. One in particular, in New Zealand, involves her acceptance of a traditional Maori challenge *above*.

Her Majesty has also met with widely varying weather conditions when in New Zealand but, despite this, two things have always remained constant, namely the crowd's eagerness to meet and greet their Queen, and her eagerness to exchange a few words with as many of them as possible. (Serge Lemoine)

In Brisbane, Australia, the Queen was met by a group of Scouts and Guides *left* before she walked through the streets accompanied by the Lord Mayor, Alderman F.N. Sleeman *above left*.

Still in Australia, the Queen pictured in Freemantle *above,* and in Darwin *right and far right*.

Her Majesty pictured *left* at a State dinner in Papua, New Guinea and *above* at the Royal Opera House, Covent Garden, where she attended a Gala Jubilee performance of opera and ballet.

The Queen and Princess Margaret *above* with the Duke of Beaufort's hounds and *right* Her Majesty with the Queen Mother at a cross-country equestrian event. (Serge Lemoine).

Overleaf. President Carter and President Giscard d'Estaing, who were in London for the Downing Street Summit, pictured with the Queen in the Blue Drawing Room at Buckingham Palace.

Pages 274 and 275. From the left: Pierre Trudeau (Canada), Takeo Fukada (Japan), Princess Margaret, James Callaghan, Prince Charles, Giscard d'Estaing (France), The Queen, The Queen Mother, President Carter (USA), Giulio Andreotti (Italy), Prince Philip and Helmut Schmidt (West Germany) in the Blue Drawing Room at Buckingham Palace.

Pageantry was very much in evidence in Scotland when the Queen arrived in Edinburgh. Under misty skies, in front of thousands of people, the massed bands of Pipes and Drums Beat the Retreat *below and right.*
On her arrival at St Giles' Cathedral *below right* Her Majesty was met by a Guard of Honour from the Scottish Regiments. (Serge Lemoine).

The Queen arriving in Scotland *overleaf* at the start of her Silver Jubilee visit. (Serge Lemoine).

The Queen's Silver Jubilee celebrations provided her with more opportunities to meet and talk to ordinary people than had ever been possible previously.
The pictures on these pages show the happy reactions of the people and, indeed, of the Queen during walkabouts in Perth, Scotland, *top left*, where a patriotic Pekingese managed to secure an unusally fine vantage point *top right*.

Her Majesty talking to children in Edinburgh *left* and in Glasgow *right*.

The Queen riding in the Scottish Coach *left* during her Jubilee tour of Scotland.

Her Majesty delivering her speech *top* to the dignitaries of the Church of Scotland and *above* leaving St. Giles' Cathedral with the Duke of Edinburgh.

Driving in State Coaches through the streets of Edinburgh are the Queen and Prince Philip *top right*, and Prince Charles and the Queen Mother *right*.

Wearing the robes of the Order of the Thistle, the Queen Mother, the Queen and Prince Philip and Prince Charles leaving St Giles' Cathedral. (All pictures: Serge Lemoine).

The Queen and the Duke of Edinburgh at a garden party *above, below and left* they gave in the gardens of Holyroodhouse for the dignitaries of Edinburgh and at which the Queen spent nearly two hours with her guests. (Serge Lemoine).

A cup being presented *right* by the Queen to the winners of youth group displays at Meadowbank Stadium, Edinburgh. (Serge Lemoine).

The Gold State Coach, *overleaf and pages 290 and 291* pulled by eight Windsor Greys, carries the Queen and Prince Philip en route for St Paul's Cathedral for the Silver Jubilee Thanksgiving Service. (Serge Lemoine).

The Silver Jubilee Thanks-giving Service in St. Paul's Cathedral, and the extended walkabout on the way to lunch at the Guildhall were just two of the events of Jubilee Day that were shared by millions of people, both in the United Kingdom and abroad, through the medium of television. The cameras saw the Queen and other members of the Royal Family in fittingly solemn mood during the actual service *right and far right, top* and then gradually relaxing as they left the cathedral *left*. The Queen was obviously delighted by her reception on her way to the Guildhall, so much so that the walk took considerably longer than had been anticipated – there were so many people to speak to and so many posies to accept *bottom left*.

The Duke and Duchess of Kent and their children the Earl of St. Andrews, Lady Helen Windsor and Lord Nicholas Windsor, together with Prince Michael of Kent, Princess Alexandra and Lord Mountbatten leaving St. Paul's Cathedral *right* after the thanksgiving service.

Overleaf. The splendid scene in St Paul's Cathedral during the Silver Jubilee Thanksgiving Service. (Serge Lemoine).

The delight of the Queen as she accepted gifts of flowers, and the sincere congratulations of the crowds in London, on Jubilee Day, is evident from her expression in the charming pictures *left and above.*

The biggest crowds since the Coronation lined the Mall as the Queen rode in procession at the Trooping the Colour Ceremony in Jubilee Year *right.*

Overleaf and pages 300 and 301. The Queen making her speech at the Jubilee luncheon in the Guildhall.

Appearances by the Royal Family on the balcony of Buckingham Palace have, for many years, been a feature of great occasions. Huge crowds gather outside the palace gates chanting "We want the Queen" and, when she obliges them and steps onto the balcony it seems that the roar that greets her must be heard all over London. Each time the Queen and her family go back inside the palace the chant starts up again, and the whole process is repeated many times.

When the Queen walked from St. Paul's Cathedral to the Guildhall on Jubilee Day the waiting crowds had an opportunity to see one of the most attractive outfits *right* she wore during the whole of Jubilee Year.

Various personalities were presented to the Queen when she attended a performance of the Royal Windsor Big Top Show in Billy Smart's circus tent in Home Park *above*.

Left. Her Majesty the Queen acknowledges the salutes of ships in the Mersey during her visit to Liverpool. (Serge Lemoine).

The Queen and Prince Philip *right* in Ipswich during the Eastern England Silver Jubilee tour.

At Butterley Hall, near Chesterfield, the Queen was presented with a doll *overleaf* as she walked among the crowds in a sports field.

A page of pictures illustrating some of the many engagements the Queen was pleased to fulfil during Silver Jubilee Year.

Her Majesty in St. Mawes, Cornwall *top left*; at an evening of entertainment provided for her in Manchester *centre left*; driving along the course at the Devon and Exeter steeplechase meeting at Haldon, in the West Country, with the Duke of Edinburgh *bottom left*; being presented with posies in a library in Mansfield *far right bottom,* and in the streets of Mansfield *above,* where she made an extensive walkabout *right.*

During her Jubilee walkabout in Derby, the Queen was presented with a gift by this young admirer *top left*. Just prior to the walkabout she had presented *left* a charter conferring city status on the town.

Eager young residents, cameras and flags at the ready *above* greet Her Majesty during her Jubilee visit to Dudley, and when she made her two-day tour of the West Midlands, she accepted a floral tribute *left* from a group of children in Birmingham's Victoria Square.

311

Far left top, and near right top. The Queen during a walkabout in Haverfordwest.

The Queen walking among the people of Carmarthen, *far left centre,* and waving to them, *near left, top,* after signing the Golden Book of the town.

Far left, bottom. At the end of her visit to Caerphilly castle, the Queen was presented with a posy of flowers by local children.

Bottom centre. Dignitaries being presented to the Queen on her arrival at Lancaster Station.

Below. A farewell wave from an aircraft of the Queen's Flight, as Her Majesty takes her leave after the Jubilee Royal Air Force review at R.A.F. Finningley.

During her Silver Jubilee walkabout in the Commercial Road shopping precinct in Portsmouth, the Queen was presented with posies by local children *left*.

There was a great welcome for the Queen on her arrival *above* at Caerphilly castle.

Overleaf left. Twenty-five children, one for each year of her reign, greeted the Queen when she arrived at Caerphilly Castle in Wales. More presentations of posies *overleaf right* also in the Commercial Road shopping precinct in Portsmouth.

In Silver Jubilee Year the Queen, aboard the Royal Yacht Brittania, reviewed the fleet at Spithead. The Ark Royal's company was drawn up on the deck of the aircraft carrier *above* as the Brittania passed.

After reviewing the fleet the Queen visited Portsmouth, and she is pictured with the crowd in Guildhall Square *above left*.

Reviews, not surprisingly, played a considerable part in the ceremonies that took place during Silver Jubilee Year. At the review of the Royal Air Force at RAF Finningley the Queen and the Duke of Edinburgh drove in an open field car along the lines of aircraft and crews *left*.

The last engagement carried out by Her Majesty during her Silver Jubilee tour of the United Kingdom was a visit to Northern Ireland in August 1977. The whole of her visit, including her speech, which was made at the University of Coleraine, was the subject of a rapturous welcome, providing a fitting end to Her Majesty's 'Royal Progress'.

(All pictures: Serge Lemoine).

First published in Great Britain 1978 by Colour Library International Ltd.
© Illustrations: Colour Library International/Camera Press/Serge Lemoine.
Colour Separations by La Cromolito, Milan, Italy.
Display and text filmsetting by Focus Photoset, London, England.
Printed and bound by L.E.G.O. Vicenza, Italy.
All rights reserved.
ISBN 0-8317-7520-3
MAYFLOWER BOOKS.